GIS in Site Design

GIS in Site Design

NEW TOOLS FOR DESIGN PROFESSIONALS

Karen C. Hanna
R. Brian Culpepper

John Wiley & Sons, Inc.

New York ▪ Chichester ▪ Weinheim ▪ Brisbane ▪ Singapore ▪ Toronto

Library of Congress Cataloging-in-Publication Data:
Hanna, Karen C.
    GIS in site design / Karen C. Hanna, R. Brian Culpepper.
       p.   cm.
    Includes index.
    ISBN 0-471-16387-2 (pbk. : alk. paper)
    1. Landscape design—Computer programs.   2. Geographic information systems.   I. Culpepper, R. Brian.   II. Title.
SB472.45.H348   1998
712'.3'0285574—dc21   97-39471

CONTENTS

This book is a response to 25 years in the design profession of landscape architecture and to some disturbing trends I have observed during that time. I have seen landscape architects relinquish their position at the forefront of GIS application, and, in so doing, they have lost much of their impact on the environmental half of our twofold paradigm: design and nature.

In 1972 I was working for the firm of Royston, Hanamoto, Beck and Abey in San Francisco. The West Coast was experiencing a small recession, which of course had an impact on the construction industry, thus reducing the design work load in the office. In response to this reduction, RHBA pursued and won contracts for some planning projects. The first of these with which I was involved was the *Smith River Highway Visual Analysis Study.* Under the watchful eye of Asa Hanamoto, Gene Kunit, my colleague and coauthor, and I developed some innovative approaches to the use of computers in visual analysis. We worked with an outside computer consultant, William Miller, of Los Angeles, who truly delivered more than he thought he had bargained for. That report won a national American Society of Landscape Architects (ASLA) Merit Award, and the client, the U.S. Forest Service, republished it as its handbook of visual analysis.

That study was followed by *Recreation and Open Space Elements of the General Plan for the County of Santa Barbara.* The state of California had mandated all its counties to produce general plans, each including nine separate elements, all of which were due in Sacramento by June 1975. The County of Santa Barbara decided that its general plan would be developed using a computerized database. Our outside consultant was Environmental Systems Research Institute (ESRI), then located in San Francisco. The biggest job for this organization was inputting the data. There were no shared databases at that time, so each project required that we generate our own. Many times a database would be used for a single project. Again, we experimented with various computer models, with data structures that led to finer grid cells in the urban areas, and we pasted the not-very-interesting computer output into contour maps of adjacent areas to make more interesting graphics.

By today's standards those reports were extremely crude, but the work was very exciting. Other landscape architects and planners were hard at work at the University of California at Berkeley, Harvard's Graduate School of Design, the University of Massachusetts at Amherst, and the University of Wisconsin at Madison, developing what would come to be known as geographic information systems (GIS).

From 1975 to 1990 my landscape architecture career took many turns, mostly away from planning and toward site-specific design. In 1987, while living in San Diego, I founded my own design firm. That business, Land Design of San Diego, had public and private clients and a variety of project types. The size of those projects varied from less than an acre to a thousand acres. My staff and I designed a number of public parks, streetscapes, new home models, and erosion control plans for manufactured slopes in subdivisions. As a small business owner, I had to face many of the issues addressed in this book, including the dilemma of investing in CADD.

The audience for this book includes small and large design firms, as well as university faculty and students. The book is designed to be a user-friendly first step in exploring GIS. My hope is that it will intrigue readers with the possibilities of GIS and excite them enough to embrace this tool. I believe that my perspective is unique, because at one time or another I have been among each of the groups identified as the audience.

Currently I am a faculty member in the Landscape Architecture Department at the University of Arkansas. Because the job market in this part of the country is good and, I would like to think, in part due to the solid education we offer, our graduates find work quite readily, and most of them move into positions of responsibility in a short period of time.

Many of our students and graduates want work that addresses environmental and planning issues to a much greater extent. Coming from a rural region encompassing small towns and much natural beauty, many of them want to protect the heritage with which they grew up, and they are frustrated to see a political structure that ignores the environment and designers who are more concerned with office management than with societal issues. These are the students who take the three GIS courses currently offered on our campus and all the ecology courses they can find. However, most of the firms they will work for are not set up to pursue design or planning from this perspective.

Finally, as a graduate student, in the early 1990s I decided to tackle the issue of designers who are left out of GIS because it is so alien to them. In the early 1970s we had used suitability mapping to produce the results we needed. That system had worked well enough for planning, but it was awkward for designing. The fact that everything had to be converted to a numeric rating bothered me. The final maps told a story, but we weren't always exactly sure what story, at least not in every part of the study area. I could see that planners were comfortable with the suitability maps most of the time, but designers were always asking, "What's going on over here; why is this area so dark?" Designers are very literal in this regard, and while suitability maps are great for policy-making, they are not so great for place making.

The process documented in Chapter 10 grew out of my graduate thesis. I performed the computer maneuvers at the Center for Advanced Spatial Technologies (CAST) at the University of Arkansas. Through an introduction by CAST's director, Dr. Fred Limp, I was able to present my technique to the National Park Service. Since 1994 two Civil War battlefield master plans have been generated using this technique. My coauthor on this book, Brian Culpepper, worked with me on those battlefield design projects, and we are now preparing a video documenting this process, also for the National Park Service. I am fairly confident in saying that the people we have worked with at the National Park Service like this approach, as do their local partners at the Arkansas Department of Parks and Tourism and the Oklahoma Historical Society.

My only hesitation in writing this book is that it will fall into the wrong hands. The process detailed here is not as simple as it may appear. Education and experience must precede the act of site designing, whether in a GIS, with suitability mapping, or with the graphic method I have devised. Site design represents the point where theory actually meets the earth. The consequences of construction are difficult to reverse, so site designers accept a tremendous responsibility in placing facilities, especially on virgin ground.

Brain Culpepper has been responsible for all the computer applications and output you will see in this work. He is the one who set up the files, performed the analytical operations, did trouble-shooting when the computer or its several peripherals took short vacations, and wordlessly made changes at my request. I think of him as a GIS wizard, and I could not have completed this book or the National Park Service battlefield projects without him. Some of the recent innovations have been his, and he is a wonderful spokesman for GIS in the design professions.

As with any project, some decisions are based on budget. Brian and I made the decision to print black-and-white images in this book so that a CD could be provided for the color images. The final site analysis and terrain drape images are much more legible on the computer screen or as slides than they are in print. We have designed the CD to be a much-shortened version of parts of the book, so it can stand alone. We ask for your indulgence with the gray scale images printed herein.

The reader may realize that most of the experience described here and throughout the book is mine, not Brian's. Many parts of the book are written in the first person, and that person is I. When the plural *we* is used, it refers to both Brian and me. Again, I ask your indulgence in this literary anomaly.

It was quite an honor to be asked to write this book. It is not often that one gets an opportunity to put years of thought and work into print. I hope this book will give its readers insights that will improve their work as well.

Karen C. Hanna

So many people have been instrumental in bringing this project to completion. My involvement with GIS techniques began in the early seventies, while I worked at Royston, Hanamoto, Beck and Abey in San Francisco. My colleagues at that time included Asa Hanamoto and Eugene Kunit. They certainly had an influence on this book.

Much more recently, my graduate advisory committee helped me frame and explore the GIS graphic technique which I present here. Dr. Malcolm Cleaveland headed the committee, which also included Dr. Fred Limp, Dr. John Dixon and Professor John Crone.

The greatest assistance has been provided by the people at the Center for Advanced Spatial Technologies (CAST). These are the most intelligent, dedicated, down-to-earth, and helpful people with whom I have ever worked. My coauthor, Brian Culpepper, was trained as a landscape architect, but he has become one of the technically gifted GIS experts at CAST. CAST is led by two brilliant men, Fred Limp and Jim Farley. Both have played essential roles in this and other of my publications. Others who have willingly helped me at one time or another include Bob Harris, Shelby Johnson, Malcolm Williamson, Rob Dzur, James Sullins and Mike Garner. Paula Justus and Karen Wagner have often provided information related to the National Park Service grants which served as the impetus for much of this work. I am especially grateful to those CASTers who reviewed chapters of this book, some on very short notice.

Two colleagues who reviewed chapters are Walt Bremer, at Cal Poly, San Luis Obispo, and David Hulse, at University of Oregon. I am very grateful for their input on this book and other GIS discussions we have had over the years. Steve Ervin of Harvard's Graduate School of Design has provided encouragement on several occasions.

Over the past several years the National Park Service has asked me to prepare master plans for two civil war battlefield parks: one at Prairie Grove, Arkansas, and one at Honey Springs, Oklahoma. Through that research I was able to perfect this technique. From NPS I am grateful to Jan Townsend, and her successor, Bryan Mitchell, Rebecca Shrimpton, Ginger Carter and Maureen Foster. From the Arkansas Department of Parks and Tourism I would like to thank Greg Butts, Stan Graves, Todd Ferguson, and Rex Friedman. At Prairie Grove Battlefield State Park I am especially indebted to Ed Smith and Don Montgomery. The Oklahoma Historical Society was instrumental in the Honey Springs Project. I am grateful to Dr. Bill Lees, Mr. Ralph Jones, and Mr. Richard Ryan for their help.

During 1997 I conducted a phone survey which is summarized in Chapter Eight. From landscape architecture, planning, and engineering firms, and from government agencies, a total of eighteen individuals shared their GIS insights with me. I am grateful that they were willing to take the time to participate.

At the School of Architecture at the University of Arkansas I would like to thank the dean, Dan Bennett, for all the ways he has facilitated my GIS research work and made allowances for the time needed to complete this book. Within the Department of Landscape Architecture I would like to thank the faculty who reviewed chapters: John Crone, Judy Brittenum and Frank Burggraf. My deepest thanks go to my talented secretary, Judy Stone, who surfed the Net and screened calls on my behalf. Finally, Mary Comstock, a Ph.D. candidate in English did the final proof reading before I submitted the manuscript.

At John Wiley I would like to thank Tracy Thornblade, Dan Sayre, Janet Feeney, Amanda Miller and Katherine Gayle.

Finally, I must thank my family for all the support and encouragement they've given me over the years. In the brightest and darkest hours, they were always there.

Karen C. Hanna

A very sincere thanks to an excellent teacher, friend, and landscape architect who sparked my interest in this "GIS stuff" several years ago when I was a red-eyed undergraduate student. She either started me in the right direction or pushed me off a cliff! I thank you Karen, and will be forever indebted to you for your invitation to coauthor this book.

I'd like to thank my "coaches" and coworkers, past and present, at the Center for Advanced Spatial Technologies (CAST), at the University of Arkansas, Fayetteville. A special thanks to two gifted leaders, Dr. Fred Limp and Jim Farley, as well as the rest of the CAST crew—Shelby D. Johnson, Rob Dzur, Mike Garner, Bruce Gorham, Dan Puckett, James Sullins, Karen Wagner, Malcolm Williamson, Debbie Harmon, Paula Justus, Anne Gisiger, Don Catanzaro, Eben Cooper, Bob Harris, Stephan Pollard, Pam Styles, Rick Thompson, Joe Bellas, Mark Wiggins, Shelley McGinnis, Glenn Barton, Galen Denham, and Wang Song—for making work so interesting, challenging, and enjoyable during the past five years. I could not ask for a better group of friends and colleagues.

My most sincere thanks goes to my family, but especially my Mom, Dad, and brother, Chris, who continue to encourage and support me, fully, as I travel this winding road called "life." I love you, guys. Thank you, Linda, for the gift of time and understanding.

My appreciation to the University of Arkansas, Fayetteville, for preparing me for my chosen profession, landscape architecture. More particularly, thanks to my many friends and colleagues in the University's School of Architecture and College of Arts and Sciences. I offer sincere gratitude to all of the faculty and visiting faculty of these two departments.

At the National Park Service's American Battlefield Protection Program and CR-GIS Washington, D.C., office, I am very grateful to Pat Tiller, Maureen Foster, Ginger Carter, John Kneorl, Katie Ryan, Bonnie Burns, Rebecca Shrimpton, and Jan Townsend for their assistance and effort over the past few years and for making this research possible. Greg Butts, Stan Graves, Todd Ferguson, and Rex Friedman of the Arkansas Department of Parks and Tourism, also deserve a thank you for moving our research into practice and protecting one of our nation's most treasured historic sites. The Oklahoma Historical Society and the Friends of the Honey Springs Battlefield share their vision, and I am grateful to Dr. Bill Lees, Mr. Ralph Jones, and Mr. Richard Ryan for their help at the Honey Springs Battlefield.

I must thank Tracy Thornblade, Day Sayre, Janet Feeney, Amanda Miller, and Katherine Gayle at John Wiley & Sons, Inc., for their collective efforts on behalf of this book. A special thanks to Mary Comstock for the final proof reading before submission.

Finally, to all of my friends and colleagues who continue to enrich my life and sometimes, actually, laugh at my jokes. Thank You!

R. Brian Culpepper

How and Why

This book answers two questions: "How would I?" and "Why should I?"

It is written for the disciplines of landscape architecture, land planning, urban planning, civil engineering, architecture, environmental planning, and any other group involved in site design or multipurpose land planning. It is written for private practitioners, design professionals who work in agencies, university professors, undergraduate and graduate students.

This book is neither a text nor a comprehensive reference, but it identifies many good reference sources. It is a brief introduction to the general world of Geographic Information Systems (GIS), and it presents a new approach to the use of GISs that makes them more accessible to the design professionals previously named.

Each chapter gives an overview of the topic, concentrating on those elements that one will need to know in order to begin an intelligent conversation with:

A computer hardware salesman,
A GIS software trainer or technician,
A data distributor,
A potential GIS client, or
An office manager.

The new approach has been developed to correspond to the design process most of us were taught in college and that many of us still use in practice. However, it differs from standard GIS models that have been in use since the 1960s. This is a commonsense approach, using the computer in the same way we have worked for decades with tracing paper and markers. The results are worth the effort, and the effort is not that great. You don't need a degree in math or logic, you don't need to add long hours to your workweek, you will follow the same thought process you have always followed, and you will be very pleased with your "smart maps."

Besides "how," we will also discuss "why." Why use GIS at all? Many people think it is complex, expensive, and too crude for site work. None of those concerns is true any longer. The software has become easier to learn, easier to use, less expensive, and it can be operated on a PC or a Macintosh. No longer do we have to invest in expensive workstations and hire computer specialists to operate them. The technology has become much more accessible to the average design office.

Why should design professionals get involved in GIS? Not everyone should. If your practice consists primarily of custom residential properties or sculpture gardens, maybe GIS is not for you. If your practice includes land planning of any sort, recreation planning, open space planning, or visual resource analysis; if it includes the design of large sites such as subdivisions, golf courses, parks, campuses or the design of linear systems such as greenways, trails, or riparian restoration, then GIS is a good tool for you to use. Much of this planning and design work is currently being done by engineering firms because they can meet clients' needs to employ GIS data and deliver products in a GIS environment. GIS is just a tool, nothing more. If you can make good use of GIS, there is no reason that you should not have the tool at your disposal.

In the beginning of GIS technology, before it was called GIS, landscape architects were at the leading edge. Over the decades they have turned their attention back to traditional design methods, and other professionals have moved into this niche. Site planners, landscape architects, and other "midscale" designers need to be acquainted with this tool before certain markets are permanently off-limits to them.

GIS IN SITE DESIGN: NEW TOOLS FOR DESIGN PROFESSIONALS

Part One: What is GIS about?

1. GIS in general

2. GIS history

3. Who else uses GIS?

Part Two: What is GIS specifically?

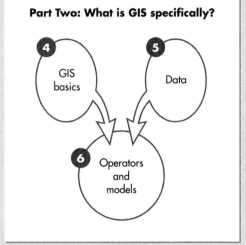

4. GIS basics

5. Data

6. Operators and models

Part Three: Designers & GIS

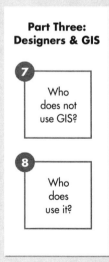

7. Who does not use GIS?

8. Who does use it?

Part Four: Adapting GIS to site design

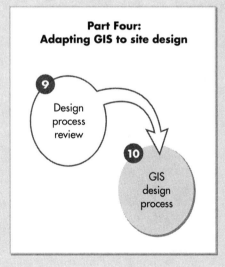

9. Design process review

10. GIS design process

Part Five: Is this for me?

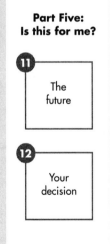

11. The future

12. Your decision

SUMMARY OF CHAPTERS

WHAT'S THIS ALL ABOUT?

Computers have changed our world so thoroughly that we are often not aware of their presence or, at other times, of their importance. Sometimes we are surprised to learn that something we took for granted or something we never thought about is affected by computer limitations or new advances.

Those of us who work in land planning, urban planning, site design, and environmental management have paradigms within which we work. Some of these are determined by our training and experience; some are shaped by the regulations of the jurisdictions in which we work; many are set by public opinion and budget concerns. Paradigms are not usually shaped by the tools of our trades. However, over time, powerful tools can so radically change the work that they allow new patterns of thought to evolve.

By themselves, Geographic Information Systems (GIS) will not create new paradigms. For the most part, whatever can be done by computer can also be done by hand. Realistically, GIS makes some operations possible that cannot be done with an army of technicians working for months on end. From that point of view, GIS is more than an incredible tool: it is a means of exploring options that otherwise could not be considered. So even if it does not lead to new types of solutions, GIS has changed the approach to planning and design and has created an elite group of land planners and site designers who have something unique to offer their clients and constituents.

In our professional lives the computer is a daily companion: we use it for report writing, cost estimating, record keeping, drafting, and map production. It is worth knowing that the computer can offer you yet another very powerful tool: smart maps. Their value may not be obvious to you now, and, indeed, your particular practice may never benefit from their use. You owe it to yourself to find out what they are before your ignorance is no longer bliss. Furthermore, this book will share a new method for using this tool, one that is tailored to the thought patterns and work habits of land planners and site designers. This book is written for the nontechnical designer and planner: you won't get lost in the jargon; you won't be confused by the objectives. It is our hope that you will appreciate what GIS can do for a project or a practice and that you will be able to make intelligent decisions about its place in your professional life.

In General, What Are Geographic Information Systems?

Geographic Information Systems (GIS) are "smart maps." They are smart because they are tied to databases and they know exactly where they are on the face of the earth. They can also perform feats such as value summation, neighborhood evaluation, and buffering.

Each of you is familiar with Computer Aided Drafting and Design (CADD) systems. These have revolutionized professional design practices over the last three decades. College graduates are expected to be familiar with their use, and CADD is so widespread in today's offices that most young professionals no longer worry about being typecast as the CADD-nerd. Most interdisciplinary files are shared in digital form now, relying on CADD to produce base drawings and final documents. CADD is the standard of the industry, just as shared databases are the standard throughout the business world.

DATABASES ARE EVERYWHERE

Databases are an integral part of our lives. Your bank account is stored in a database. Your income tax records, your medical records, your property tax records are all stored in databases. The census information you provide becomes part of an important database that is used for everything from determination of voting districts to public policy development to budget calculations (Date 1986). Your address is part of many databases, some of which are used to determine which advertising brochures you will receive in the mail. Design and maintenance of database management systems (DBMS) form a huge, sophisticated sector of commercial enterprises. All of this sophistication is available with a GIS.

CADD DRAWINGS FLOAT

CADD drawings, just like their hand-drawn predecessors, represent a somewhat flat surface somewhere on the earth, usually not too far from your own office or studio. Even though the drawings show contours to indicate changing grades on the site,

Figure 1.1   Earth.

Earth flattened.

the underlying assumption is that this site is similar to all others on earth and can be represented on a two-dimensional sheet of paper.

GIS MAPS ARE ATTACHED TO THE EARTH

GIS also produces drawings on two-dimensional sheets of paper, but within the computer the scene is very different. The GIS recognizes the curvature of the earth. It also knows the precise locations of the boundary corners (and all other points) of the site or study area on the surface of the earth. This is important when you are studying very large tracts of land and when you are importing data from many different sources. In order for you to perfectly align the various types of information, and thus yield accurate maps, the curvature of the earth must be considered and locational precision must be achieved. We will examine this in greater detail in Chapter 4.

GISs INCLUDE STOREHOUSES OF INFORMATION

Because each point on a GIS map has its own "address," it is tied to a database that can store an unlimited amount of information about that point. Advances in DBMS take their value far beyond simple retrieval of data and generation of statistics; instructions to the databases allow for examination of specific sets of conditions not immediately obvious to the user.

Most databases today are of the relational type, meaning that they are collections of tables that are logically associated by common attributes. By selecting certain record types and exclud-

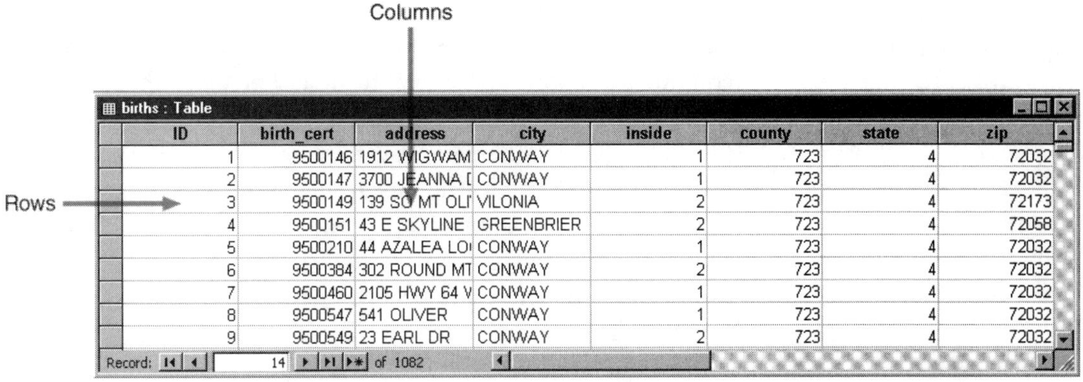

Figure 1.2   Relational database sample.

Columns

ID	birth_cert	address	city	inside	county	state	zip
1	9500146	1912 WIGWAM	CONWAY	1	723	4	72032
2	9500147	3700 JEANNA [	CONWAY	1	723	4	72032
3	9500149	139 SO MT OLI	VILONIA	2	723	4	72173
4	9500151	43 E SKYLINE	GREENBRIER	2	723	4	72058
5	9500210	44 AZALEA LOI	CONWAY	1	723	4	72032
6	9500384	302 ROUND MT	CONWAY	2	723	4	72032
7	9500460	2105 HWY 64 V	CONWAY	1	723	4	72032
8	9500547	541 OLIVER	CONWAY	1	723	4	72032
9	9500549	23 EARL DR	CONWAY	2	723	4	72032

births : Table

Rows

Record: 14 of 1082

ing others, the tables can be reconfigured, and statistics can be calculated based on any new set of parameters. Instructions can be given that select certain columns or rows and call for mathematical operations on them to determine trends, extremes, or concentrations of conditions. The sequence in which the tables are restructured can make a big difference in the resulting reports. Powerful databases are usually referred to as "robust."

All of these operations are available in a GIS because there are two complementary components: maps and databases. They reinforce one another and make the GIS environment very exciting.

Attributes Enrich the Maps

Using the GIS map component now, we will consider some of the data types that are commonly found. Each type of information is called a theme. Common themes include vegetation, soils, elevation, flood hazard, ownership, zoning, and land use. They can usually be classified as natural or cultural. The specific categories of data, within each theme, are called attributes. If *soils* is the theme, *sandy-loam* may be an attribute. The attributes are stored in the database.

Data Input, Operators, and Models

All types of basic data are collected and entered into the computer. Collection methods include site survey, aerial photos, and remote sensing. Data input methods include digitizing, scanning, and digital transference. Some data needs processing between collection and entry. Aerial photos usually require interpretation before they can be entered in a meaningful way. Remotely sensed data needs sophisticated analysis before the data can be used in a GIS. Even if data is transferred from one computer to another in digital form, at one point the basic data was entered in someone's computer. Once the data is in digital form, it is called a thematic coverage.

Other "nonbasic" themes are generated in the computer from base themes. Hypsography, the thematic name for topography, is the basis from which contours, slope, aspect, drainages, and viewsheds can be generated. The raw data is sometimes entered as contours, but frequently it is entered as spot heights, not always in a grid as surveyors use, but often in a triangulated irregular network (TIN), which looks more like a spider web with varying densities of points. Either way, as contours or spot heights, this one data set, or theme, is used to calculate the others: slope, aspect, drainage, and viewsheds inside the GIS.

Spot heights can be used to generate contours or elevation maps in the GIS. This ability to generate new maps from others is called an operation; some of these are called analytical operators. When two or more complex operations are used in sequence to perform an analysis or a synthesis of the data, the steps are referred to as a model. Modeling is a very important aspect of GIS, one that clearly sets it apart from CADD.

THINK OF GIS THIS WAY . . .

Here are some analogies for GIS. One is that the GIS map comes with its own Rolodex. When a point is selected, the Rolodex automatically gives you the address, usually expressed as coor-

Figure 1.3   This slope map was generated within the GIS using the digital elevation model as input.

dinates or as latitude and longitude. You get a precise location on the face of the globe.

Think of GIS maps as being attached to a closed circuit television. Just as a security guard has a site plan on the counter in front of him or her, the GIS has a map image on the monitor. As you select points on the map, descriptions of existing conditions appear to the side of the screen. There are even systems that link the maps to actual video clips that run in the corner of the screen, showing the physical scene at that spot. These videos are handy for utility repairs, allowing the dispatcher to decide what kinds of equipment and vehicles to send to the site.

Finally, think of the GIS databases as being all-knowing gurus in charge of the maps. You can ask, "How many acres of coastal sage scrub exist on north-facing slopes in the third district?" and the computer will say, "There are 235.4 acres, ma'am; what else would you like to know?"

REFERENCE

Date, C. J. 1986. *An Introduction to Database Systems.* Menlo Park, CA: Addison-Wesley.

2

Where Did GIS Come From? A History of GIS in Land Planning and Site Design

ENGINEERS WERE FIRST GIS USERS

Several sources agree that the first example of a crude geographic information system used for planning purposes was a transportation study done for the City of Chicago in the late 1950s (Boyce et al. 1970). Julius Fabos (1985) reports on two pioneering groups of computerized land planners: transportation engineers and water resource engineers. Because they acted so early in the development of our major urban areas, these engineers set many standards for development, not only of our major highways and reservoir systems but of cities as a whole. The legacy of urban sprawl in this country may be traced in part to the fact that these two groups had an understanding of GIS long before other types of planners did and huge construction projects were funded based on these GIS recommendations.

An earlier example of geographically based planning, although certainly not digital, is the work of Charles Eliot. As one of the premier landscape architects of the early twentieth century Eliot did several large-scale park and greenway projects based on environmental considerations. Ian McHarg notes Eliot's work as being a precursor to his own (Miller and Pardal, 1992, pg. 87). The McHarg approach is reviewed below and in Chapters 6 and 10.

UTILITIES COMPANIES

Other early users of GIS, especially as it relates to automated mapping and facilities management (AM/FM), were utilities companies. Companies in Colorado and southern California were among the first to develop automated systems for management of existing facilities and planning for future service areas (Antenucci 1991, 21).

Note: AM/FM is a type of GIS widely used by utilities companies and agencies for operations and maintenance of their infrastructure. Primarily, they record flows, trouble spots, improvements, and changes in equipment. Because the infrastructure records and maps are in a GIS environment, these suppliers can also test proposed expansions of their systems against existing conditions.

LAND PLANNERS

In the realm of land planning, one of the most important developments occurred in the mid-1960s with the work that Ian McHarg did for the Ford Foundation at the University of Pennsylvania (McHarg [1969] 1992). Even though he did not use a computer, his techniques have formed the basis of most computerized models used for land planning around the world. Although many people think of McHarg as the colorful, outspoken champion of the environment, it is his method, not his rhetoric, that revolutionized land planning.

The McHarg overlay system assigns values to themes. A particular attribute (data category) is assigned a value that is a measure of the ability of that condition to accommodate a particular use. For instance, an open field may receive a value of 8 in terms of accommodating an urban freeway, whereas a historic village may receive a value of 1 or 0. In this example, the higher value indicates a higher suitability for the particular use. Each value is then represented by a tone or shade of adhesive film (Zip-a-tone) applied to clear acetate sheets. The sheets are then assembled and laid on top of one another. The darkest composite areas show the most suitable locations for the proposed use. This process is the origin of the term *suitability mapping*. As described, McHarg did not initially use a computer for his work, but others quickly picked up the technique and adapted it to Geographic Information Systems.

THREE APPROACHES TO LAND PLANNING

Other computerized advancements took place at the Laboratory for Computer Graphics and Spatial Analysis at Harvard's Graduate School of Design. One project of special interest during this period was conducted under the direction of Charles Harris and Carl Steinitz (Belknap and Furtado 1967). The computer was put to the test of evaluating the planning approaches of three well-known land planners: two landscape architects, Ian McHarg and Phil Lewis, and a forest ecologist, Angus Hills. As graduate students, Ray Belknap, John Furtado, and Grant Jones began this analysis, and Belknap and Furtado continued it with the help of a grant from the Conservation Foundation.

Belknap and Furtado analyzed the three approaches with the computer. The importance of this work to our discussion is that Angus Hills and Phil Lewis had developed planning approaches based on integrated units such as landforms and landscape corridors. Angus Hills's units derived from landforms as defined by soil type and forest ecology. Hills's work greatly influenced the Canadian Land Inventory System (Steiner 1991, 141) Phil Lewis's corridor units were based on physical and visual landforms and their relationship to cultural needs (see also Lewis 1996). In contrast, Ian McHarg's approach was based on separate themes. The Harvard study evaluated the success of applying these approaches in a computerized environment. The most important result of their analysis may have been the finding that each planning approach was capable of being examined in a computerized environment. The term GIS did not yet exist, but the act of land planning with the aid of a computer was clearly established by the mid-1960s.

COLLABORATION WITH SCIENTISTS

At about this time, Julius Fabos and his colleagues at the University of Massachusetts, Amherst, were developing the Met-Land planning system. This too is a computerized approach to planning. Its primary feature is the integrated use of models developed by a number of related disciplines, including clima-

Figure 2.1 *An example of a GIS study prepared in 1974 by the firm of RHBA, San Francisco, CA, for Santa Barbara County. Note the primitive computer symbols and the hybrid of computer and paste-up graphics.*

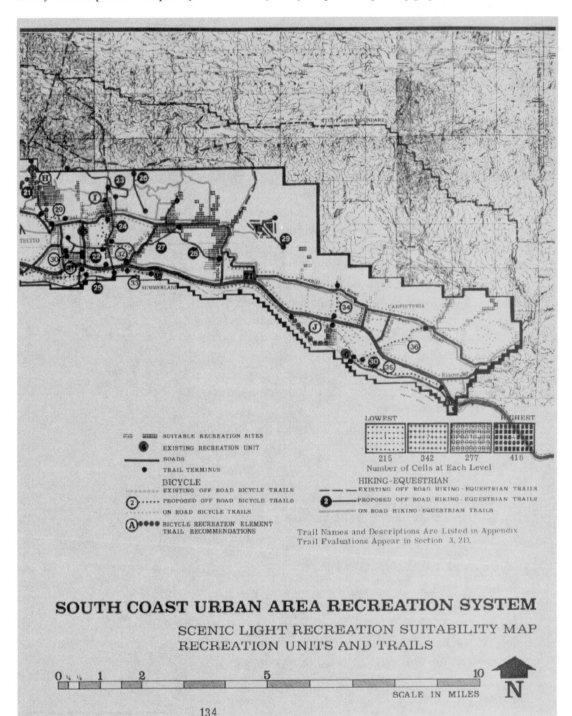

SOUTH COAST URBAN AREA RECREATION SYSTEM

SCENIC LIGHT RECREATION SUITABILITY MAP
RECREATION UNITS AND TRAILS

tology, ecology, economics, geology, forestry, wildlife biology, civil engineering, and others (Fabos and Caswell 1977). Fabos's approach is similar to Ian McHarg's in that natural and cultural themes are used as distinct layers of data. The difference is that instead of using a simple value assignment of suitability for each theme, each specialist develops for his or her own discipline an algorithmic model to achieve a very special output and these are combined in various ways to develop planning solutions. The Massachusetts Agricultural Experiment Station has published a series of reports developed within this paradigm.

MILITARY RESEARCH AND DEVELOPMENT

The defense agencies of the United States have been responsible for many of the technical advances in the field of GIS. Some of these, such as collection of satellite imagery, remote sensing, photo interpretation, and global positioning systems (GPS), have proved extremely beneficial to site designers and land planners. Because the military relies on diverse technologies for intelligence gathering, it is anticipated that its various agencies will continue to fund GIS research and development.

The U.S. Army Corps of Engineers Research Laboratory (USACERL) are responsible for development of public domain software known as GRASS (Geographic Resources Analysis Support System). This software was initially developed to determine where to hold training exercises without doing irreparable harm to the land at Fort Hood, Texas. For many years, GRASS was the only GIS software some planners and academicians could afford, and many early and recent studies in a variety of fields utilized it.

HARDWARE METAMORPHOSIS, SOFTWARE EVOLUTION

The advances made in digital technologies in the last 20 years will be the stuff of lore. These decades will be carefully studied by future historians, anthropologists, and industrialists. For our purposes, the important advances have been those that make the computer more accessible to us:

- Development of high-level computer languages that make programs easier to write

- Development of graphic user interfaces so we have fewer commands to learn
- Computers the average citizen can afford
- Much more powerful computers, with greater storage capacity, so we can accomplish more complicated tasks with apparent ease

GIS, CADD, AND THE ENVIRONMENTAL INTERFACE

As with most modern software, GIS applications continue to become more user friendly and less costly. The interface between CADD products and GIS software is dissolving. Not only does this make it easier to import CADD files as data sources, it also improves interaction with other disciplines. The ability to export GIS files to CADD streamlines the planning-to-site-design-to-construction transition that has formed the rift between planning and design for some time.

One of the leaders in developing user-friendly GIS software is ESRI (Environmental Systems Research Institute), headquartered in Redlands, California. Jack Dangermond, founder and president of ESRI, is also trained as a landscape architect. ESRI offers a whole suite of GIS packages; one of the current favorites of designers is ArcView (see Chapter 8 survey).

Other important GIS packages used by land planners, landscape architects, cities, and counties include the following (Rajani 1995):

- MGE, Modular GIS Environment, and Geomedia from Intergraph Corporation, based in Huntsville, Alabama
- MapInfo, based in Troy, New York
- Genasys, based in Fort Collins, Colorado
- AutoWorld, by AutoDesk of San Rafael, California

Other important software can be used to interface with databases outside of those attached to a GIS. Image interpretation software is important for work that relies on remotely sensed data. Furthermore, there are a number of products on the market that provide data retrieval and mapping capabilities, but are not true geographic information systems. There is software for all the major hardware platforms and for all modern, powerful operating systems. Yes, there is GIS for Macintosh.

RECENT TRENDS

Over the last 10 years the computer industry at large has redefined itself with a series of benchmark innovations:

- Establishment of computing standards
- Emergence of the Internet
- Vastly improved data availability
- Development of metadata (data specs)
- Graphic user interfaces
- True desktop publishing

All of these advances make the computer in general, and GIS specifically, more accessible for land planning and site design. This book explores each of these advances and their impacts on the design professions.

MY MOTIVATION

The sad reality is that in the early 1970s landscape architects and planners were at the forefront of GIS development and use. Over the last two and a half decades, however, we have drifted away from the big picture, and the scientists and engineers have held the GIS spotlight. To be effective as designers and advocates for the environment, we need all the tools we can get, and GIS is certainly one we need.

REFERENCES

Antenucci, John C., Kay Brown, Peter L. Croswell, and Michael J. Kevany. 1991. *Geographic Information Systems: A Guide to the Technology.* New York: Van Nostrand Reinhold.

Belknap, Raymond K., and John G. Furtado. 1967. *Three Approaches to Environmental Resource Analysis.* Washington, DC: The Conservation Foundation.

Boyce, David E., Norman D. Day, and Chris McDonald. 1970. *Metropolitan Plan Making: An Analysis of Experience with the Preparation and Evaluation of Alternative Land Use and Transportation Plan.* Philadelphia: Regional Science Research Institute.

Fabos, Julius Gy. 1985. *Land-Use Planning: From Global to Local Challenge.* New York: Chapman and Hall.

Fabos, Julius Gy, and Stephanie J. Caswell. 1977. *Composite Landscape Assessment: Assessment Procedures for Special Resources, Hazards and Development Suitability.* Part 2 of *The Metropolitan Landscape Planning Model (METLAND).* Amherst: Massachusetts Agricultural Experiment Station, University of Massachusetts.

Lewis, Philip, Jr. 1996. *Tomorrow by Design.* New York: John Wiley & Sons.

McHarg, Ian. [1969] 1992. *Design with Nature.* Garden City, NY: Natural History Press. Reprint, New York: John Wiley & Sons.

Miller, E. Lynn, and Sidonio Pardal. 1992. *Classic McHarg.* Lisbon, Portugal: CESUR, Technical University of Lisbon.

Rajani, Purvi. 1995. "Kings of the Global GIS Jungle: Key Players Push Geographic Information Technology into Mainstream Markets." *GIS World* (Fort Collins, CO), November.

Steiner, Frederick. 1991. *The Living Landscape.* New York: McGraw Hill.

Who Else Uses GIS?

Many segments of our population have been using GIS for decades. Perhaps the most widespread use is in local government. Public works departments in all our major cities, most midsize cities, and even some small towns use GIS to record and monitor street repairs, water and sewer lines, and property records. Many county clerks use GIS to assist in keeping records of title transfers, easements, tax assessments, and tax payments for estimating future tax revenues. There are also a great many more users of GIS.

Who else uses Geographic Information Systems (GIS) on a regular, even daily, basis? The U.S. military, the U.S. Forest Service, the National Park Service, the Bureau of Land Management, the U.S. Department of Fish and Wildlife, the Army Corps of Engineers, the Environmental Protection Agency, many state-level departments of transportation and natural resources, most utility companies, all major cities, and many counties (Huxhold and Martin 1996; Antenucci et al. 1991). The Federal Interagency Committee on Digital Cartography (FICDC) coordinates and reports on the use of GIS among the 62 federal agencies it oversees. In 1990, 18 federal agencies used GIS on a regular basis (Antenucci et al. 1991, 35).

It should come as no surprise that the Defense Mapping Agency of the Department of Defense uses GIS for intelligence gathering and defense strategy planning, but much of this information is classified. The military also uses GIS to decide where to hold training exercises, with goals that include protecting vegetation and sensitive habitat, preventing soil erosion, and protecting against hazardous contamination (Wager 1996). GIS is being used to design former military bases for conversion to private uses (Sherman 1995). When considering expansion of

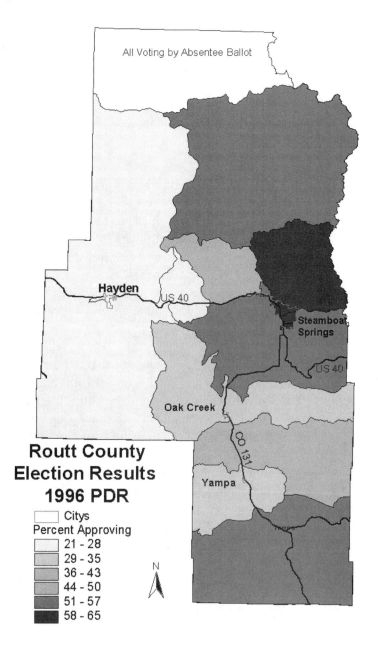

Figure 3.1   Political map of Routt County, CO.

existing or installation of new airports, the Federal Aviation Administration uses GIS to determine the impacts of noise levels in residential areas and at sensitive facilities such as hospitals (O'Connor 1995).

State departments of transportation use GIS to predict and schedule highway maintenance contracts by recording previous repairs, traffic loads, and weather conditions (Pieper 1996). GIS allows them to estimate future costs, assign manpower, and order materials. New highway routing relies heavily on GIS, using McHargian suitability mapping and other approaches (Smith 1997; Springer 1996).

States and municipalities use GIS for emergency and service routing. Network analysis is a GIS function that suggests optimum routes for emergency response, city and school bus deployment, and garbage collection. Factors such as rush hour traffic and current accidents can be input to adjust the suggested route. Municipal police departments, 911 services, ambulance companies, and fire departments, as well as public and private transit companies, use network analysis to route their vehicles (Elliott 1997; Sedgwick and Gilley 1996).

Political parties use GIS to analyze voting patterns. Voting districts are configured using GIS analysis in combination with census data. Court districts and school districts are reapportioned based on GIS analysis.

Agriculture uses GIS in a number of ways. Pest distribution patterns have been studied using GIS (Schell and Lockwood 1995). Aerial photography and remote sensing are used as data input for estimating crop yields and determining water usage within irrigation districts (Lang 1996).

When a global positioning system (GPS) is combined with GIS, "precision farming" is possible. Precision farming allows farmers to monitor fertilizer needs and apply such materials in an extremely controlled manner. The process begins with soil samples, coupled with readings of their precise locations made by GPS. Analysis of the samples gives precise fertilizer application rates for each sector of a field. A special farm vehicle equipped with a GPS and a computer applies the prescribed amount of fertilizer to each area. During each of the following four years, crop yields for each part of the field are measured either with monitoring devices on the harvesters or by aerial photos. The yield is used as an index of the amount of nutrients used by the plants and, thus, the amount remaining in the soil. New calculations are made for refertilizing, and precise amounts are applied each year. Every fifth year new soil samples are taken, and the cycle is repeated. Precision farming not only saves money on fertilizer applications, but dramatically reduces dangerous runoff (Medders 1996).

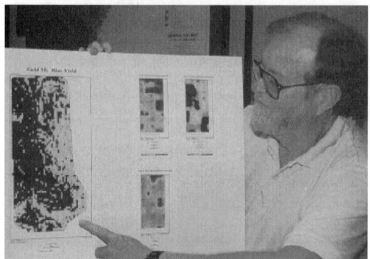

Figure 3.2 Precision farming utilizes GPS monitoring devices attached to harvesting equipment and GIS analysis to apply highly accurate amounts of fertilizer to agricultural fields.

Utilities companies use GIS extensively. Whether its application is used for electricity, telephone, water, sewer, storm drains, or natural gas, GIS plays a vital role in their distribution and delivery systems management, as well as in expansion planning (Utsler 1997). Water impoundment agencies use GIS to monitor storm events and subsequent runoff in an effort to regulate dams and reduce flood damage. Electric companies use GIS to monitor usage and available power supplies in order to distribute power and avoid outages. Deregulation of the utilities will bring about many new facilities projects, which will generate environmental assessment and planning work (Black 1997).

Retailers and franchisers use GIS to target advertising campaigns and to locate new stores. The ready availability of census data, combined with tract and district information, allows demographic and geographic input for many types of marketing analyses ("Awards of Merit" 1996). Franchisers can locate concentrations of their ideal customers based on income levels, education, family size, and ethnicity, using census data that is available at a nominal charge from the Census Bureau.

The Bureau of the Census has been one of the leaders in the development of GIS technology. The Bureau maintains two main files: the data itself is kept on Summary Tape Files (STF). The geographic component file was first called DIME (Dual Independent Map Encoding) and is now called TIGER (Topologically Integrated Geographically Encoded and Referenced). TIGER files can be obtained directly from the Census Bureau for a nominal fee or from a variety of service agencies, some of which improve the files before reselling them. Most of these service agencies check for errors and omissions, add labels, update files, and improve accuracy.

LANDSCAPE ARCHITECTURE APPLICATIONS

The preceding examples may not be very closely related to landscape architecture, site design, or land planning, but consider the following. The National Park Service (NPS) already uses GIS for management of its heavily visited parks, for design of units such as Civil War battlefields, and to map historical artifacts (Dobson 1997; Hanna 1995; Murphy and Smith 1995).

The U.S. Forest Service uses GIS to inventory standing timber and to manage its yield (Wilson 1997). These decisions affect many recreation and visual resource issues. Although a project's landscape architect may not initiate standing timber analysis, he or she may be able to suggest alternatives to be tested in the GIS that will result in timber cuts in different locations, freeing up lands previously targeted for harvest. This alternative analysis gives the designer many more choices in use area allocations and more control of the process in general. Add the GIS viewshed operators to the equation, and the potential for improved forest use increases demonstrably.

Every major municipality, and many counties, use GIS to record property parcel information (Juhl 1994). The periodical *GIS World* (Fort Collins, CO) features a different municipality or other local government, with details on its GIS applications, in every monthly issue. In addition to governments' using GIS for infrastructure management, county clerks' offices use GIS to record property transfers, and tax assessors use it to record pay-

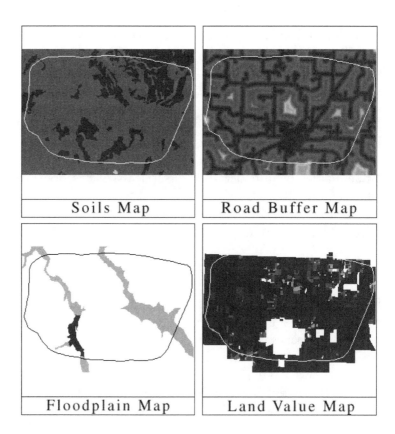

Figure 3.3   Four raster maps.

ments and estimate future revenues (Summerell and Wrenn 1997). These digital records afford not only graphic opportunities, but also greatly expanded data sources. Depending on the original design of a city's GIS, a site designer can pose queries such as "How many public swimming pools are within a five-mile radius of this park?" "How many tennis courts east of the highway are on public lands?" or "How many acres of parking exist at all the parks with lighted ballfields, and what is their average size?" Few designers know how to mine the wealth of data existing in public GISs already in place. Even more troubling is that they do not know that these questions can be asked.

Data on factors such as owner, land use, assessed value, and legal descriptions are referenced to maps showing parcel boundaries and their relationships to streets, sidewalks, rights of way, easements, and bodies of water. Many cities routinely display this information over aerial photos. This readily available resource represents a tremendous source of information for landscape architects and site designers working at a number of scales.

Why haven't land planners and site designers familiarized themselves with GIS? Chapter 7 takes a closer look at that question. Since land planners use parcel and infrastructure information quite regularly, it behooves them to be knowledgeable of the systems in which the data resides.

REFERENCES

"Awards of Merit: County Shares Wealth of GIS Data via Cable TV." 1996. *American City and County* (Exeter, PA), December.

Antenucci, John C., Kay Brown, Peter L. Croswell, Michael J. Kevany. 1996. *Geographic Information Systems, A Guide to the Technology.* New York: Van Nostrand Reinhold.

Black, James D. 1997. "Utilities Move Toward Transparent GIS." *GIS World* (Ft. Collins, CO), February.

Dobson, Jerome E. 1997. "Laboratory Plans Space/Time/Entity/ Process System." *GIS World* (Ft. Collins, CO), March.

Elliott, Bill. 1997. "Vermont Moves Forward on E-911 Rural Addressing." *GIS World* (Ft. Collins, CO), June.

Hanna, Karen C. 1995. "Prairie Grove Battlefield State Park Master Plan." Little Rock: Arkansas Department of Parks and Tourism. May.

Huxhold, William E. and Michael Martin. 1996. "GIS Guides City's Neighborhood Funding Efforts." *GIS World* (Ft. Collins, CO), June.

Juhl, Ginger M. 1994. "City Relies on GIS to Reduce Costs, Increase Productivity." *GIS World* (Ft. Collins, CO), May.

Korte, George. 1996. "GIS Industry Overview." *Point of Beginning* (Troy, MI), November.

Lang, Laura. 1996. "Geo Technology Use Grows in California Ag Community." *Earth Observation Magazine* (Aurora, CO), October.

Medders, Howell. 1996. "Space Age Tools Add Precision to Farming." *Arkansas Land and Life* (Little Rock), Summer/Fall.

Murphy, Larry E. and Timothy G. Smith. 1995. "Submerged in the Past: Mapping the Beguiling waters of Florida's Biscayne and Dry Tortugas National Parks." *Geo Info Systems* (Eugene, OR), October.

O'Connor, Mark. 1995. "The Roar of the Jets: Los Angeles Airport Bureau Develops Noise Management System." *Geo Info Systems* (Eugene, OR), July.

Pieper, David. 1996. "GIS Benefits Long-Range Facilities Planning." *GIS World* (Ft. Collins, CO), November.

Schell, Scott P. and Jeffrey Lockwood. 1995. "Spatial Analysis Optimizes Grasshopper Management." *GIS World* (Ft. Collins, CO), November.

Schulman, Richard. 1996. "Digital Raster Maps: The Missing Link in Natural Resources Management." *Earth Observation Magazine* (Aurora, CO), January.

Sedgwick, Fred and Leann Gilley. 1996. "Emergency GIS for E 911 Systems." *Earth Observation Magazine* (Aurora, CO), March.

Sherman, Michael. 1995. "Planning for Peace: Using GIS to Develop Reuse of Military Facilities." *Geo Info Systems* (Eugene, OR), March.

Smith, Lisa. 1997. "The Road Most Traveled." *Earth Observation Magazine* (Aurora, CO), June.

Springer, Jim. 1996. "GIS Moves California's Motorists Toward the 21st Century." *Earth Observation Magazine* (Aurora, CO), September.

Summerell, Ray and Jamie Wrenn. 1997. "Automation Protects Quality of GIS Data." *American City and County* (Exeter, PA), January.

Utsler, Jim. 1997. "From the Ground Up." *Microstation World* (Hunstville, AL), Spring.

Wager, Todd K. 1996. "GIS and Environmental Model Integration." *Geo Info Systems* (Eugene, OR), June.

Wilson, J. D. 1997. "Photogrammetry in the Forest: Digital Photogrammetry Improves Forestry Data Management and Analysis." *Earth Observation Magazine* (Aurora, CO), February.

WHAT, SPECIFICALLY, IS GIS?

GISs have been nicknamed smart maps. Not only do they know exactly where they are on the earth, they contain information about conditions that exist everywhere in the study area. They also have an internal awareness of distances, adjacent conditions, travel paths, and addresses. They're not intuitive, but they are smart.

Specifically, Geographic Information Systems are:

1. Data, stored in a database where it can be retrieved, questioned, or reassembled,

2. Maps, showing the exact locations of the data, and

3. Programs that

line up the maps,

correct distortion,

show three-dimensional views of the study area, and

include analytical operators that manipulate, modify, or enhance the data to yield new maps and new data.

A Closer Look at Geographic Information Systems

Before we continue, let us establish what the acronym GIS represents. In the United States, GIS stands for *Geographic Information Systems.* In Great Britain and Europe, it stands for *Geographical Information Systems.* It has sometimes been written out as *Graphic Information Systems,* although that is not a widely accepted interpretation.

One of the best definitions of GIS comes from the National Center for Geographic Information and Analysis (NCGIA 1988) headquartered in Santa Barbara, CA: "A geographic information system is a computerized data base management system for capture, storage, retrieval, analysis, and display of spatial (locationally defined) data" (in Huxhold 1991, 29).

INVESTING IN GIS

It is probably with some anguish that you remember making the decision to purchase your first CADD (Computer Aided Drafting and Design) system. You could no longer delay, because all the other offices you worked with, especially those of civil engineers, were using CADD and they expected you to give them your input in the same format. If they weren't demanding it, they at least let you know that you were not "up to speed." Or a city or county agency required submittals for plan check on disk. Or one of your clients insisted on digital output. Or it seemed that all requests for proposals were asking you to list the platform and software you used for computer-aided drafting. It was a traumatic decision because of the large cash outlay for the equipment and the software, because of the uncertainty about what system to purchase, and because of the training required for much of your staff—perhaps including you!

Signs of GIS Emergence

Geographic Information Systems are not yet ubiquitous, and perhaps they never will be. However, the ever-expanding availability of data, the ongoing levels of research and development in GIS technologies such as graphic interfaces and user-friendly software, the strengthening of linkages between GIS and global positioning systems, with database management systems, the Internet, and in-the-field monitoring devices, all lead one to believe that GIS is here to stay. As other sectors of our economy grow increasingly dependent on GIS, land planners and site designers will be out of date and working at a disadvantage if they do not embrace it.

The End of Crude Data

It is currently true that much of the available data is not at a resolution directly applicable to small-scale site design. Two things are changing: off-the-shelf data is getting better, with finer and finer resolution; and data input is getting so much easier that planners and designers can prepare their own high-resolution data much more efficiently than in the past. It has also been getting increasingly easy to import CADD files into the GIS environment, and soon there will be little outward indication of where the data originated. The proliferation of data vendors and the establishment of metadata standards have also led to greatly improved data quality.

What Cost?

At the risk of being out of date immediately, we will say that in 1997 one can obtain adequate hardware and software to engage in GIS projects for less than $10,000 (U.S.). Depending on your clients' needs and the equipment and software used by other members of your design team, you can get involved for a lot less than that. Many firms have multiple platforms and applications, but it is possible to begin with somewhat modest computers and public domain software, such as GRASS (Geographic

Analysis Resource Support System) developed by the U.S. Army Corps of Engineers Research Laboratory (USACERL). (*Note:* USACERL is no longer updating GRASS, but the basic program is still available at no charge. It is a powerful GIS package; there are lots of training manuals available, and week-long training sessions are offered at various universities.)

CADD/GIS SIMILARITIES

A number of qualities that make CADD so great also apply to GIS:

1. Information can be separated in different layers, so you can make changes to some elements and intersecting lines or other parts of the image will not be affected.
2. Because data are on separate layers, they can be displayed or printed together in different combinations at different times.
3. With the proper output device, colors and patterns can be printed or plotted that are fairly close to the image shown on the computer monitor. Colors and patterns can be changed very easily.
4. Extra copies can be generated quickly and fairly inexpensively. There's no need to hand-render another print or get another photo printed (or even to warm up the diazo machine).
5. The scale of the drawing can be changed with a few simple commands and a fresh copy produced quickly. The entire site can be printed at one scale and portions of it printed at other scales. The same drawings can be printed on large sheets of paper for public presentations and on 8½-by-11-inch paper for reports.
6. Very large sites can be stored in the computer and viewed at different scales or in pieces. Rather than taping together huge base maps and trying to find a suitable place to work on them, you can reduce large sites in the computer to be viewed in their entirety, or view portions of the site closely by using the pan and zoom operations in any CADD or GIS system.
7. The drawings and map output from CADD and GIS are consistent, crisp, and clean. There are no graphite

smudges, no erasures, no eradicator shadows, no marker streaks. The line widths are uniform, the tones are solid and consistent, the lettering is perfectly formed. Professionals and the public have come to accept the cold simplicity for which these drawings were once criticized. Computer-generated images are the current standard. Some professionals enhance computer output with colored pencils or pastels applied by hand.

8. Data can be stored and transported on disk. Professionals can transfer data between their offices without redrafting or changing formats. Data archives are much smaller, and data is preserved with greater integrity. The days of faded prints, torn photos, and water-stained mylars are behind us.

QUALITIES UNIQUE TO GIS

Several qualities set GISs apart from CADD systems: (1) geo-referencing and rectification allow the maps to be accurately fitted to the earth's surface, (2) raster and vector formats each have advantages that can be used separately or in combination, (3) attribute databases give life to the maps, (4) GIS analytical operators are able to act on the data, and thus they alter the maps in ways that facilitate analysis, and (5) used in sequence, the analytical operators create models that produce maps that represent complex existing conditions, predict conditions, or exemplify scientific algorithms. We will take a closer look at each of these GIS characteristics now.

Ellipsoids

In order to graphically represent the curved surface of our planet, ellipsoids have been developed. Although early ellipsoids were based on mathematical equations, modern ellipsoids are actually based on satellite measurements. In the United States, the most commonly used ellipsoid is NAD'83 (North American Datum, revised in 1983) (Huxhold 1991, 203; Star and Estes 1990, 98).

Once the ellipsoid has been selected, a projection must also be determined. The projection is the method used to change a three-dimensional globe into a flat map surface. The variations in projections will cause differing degrees of accuracy in measurements taken in certain directions across a map. In the United States, Lambert's conic projection is used for air navigation and meteorological charts; however, the Transverse Mercator projection is most often used for topographic maps and as a base for plane coordinate systems (Huxhold 1991, 203). Thus, most land planning GIS work uses the Transverse Mercator projection.

GEO-REFERENCING A FLAT MAP ON A ROUND EARTH

For any particular project, all GIS themes must be referenced to the same ellipsoid and projection. The task of fitting maps to an ellipsoid and a projection is called geo-referencing, and it is accomplished with simple commands to the computer whenever the data is input or imported.

RECTIFYING TO A COORDINATE SYSTEM

Next, GIS maps are referenced to a particular place on the earth by using a geodetic coordinate system. The earth's lines of latitude and longitude (Lat./Lon.) do not form a grid, but a graticule, because the lines of longitude converge at the poles. The UTM, or Universal Transverse Mercator grid system, and the State Plane Coordinate System are both rectangular grids. UTM

Figure 4.1 Projections are essentially mathematical methods for flattening the earth into a two-dimensional plane.

is used for very large areas, but a State Plane Coordinate System is easier to work with for most land planning projects. Fitting the map to a coordinate grid is called rectification, and it is accomplished by identifying known points between two themes (Davis 1996, 163). Identifiable points are selected in the same areas of both maps, then other sets of pairs at opposite ends of both maps, and they are repositioned repeatedly until the desired accuracy is achieved, as reported by the computer.

GLOBAL POSITIONING SYSTEMS AUGMENTING COORDINATES

One of the shortcomings of the State Plane Coordinate System is that the field markers are too far apart for most surveyors to use. It is difficult to input data collected by field surveys in a GIS covering large areas of land and expect to eliminate discrepancies. This problem is the reason the use of global positioning systems (GPS) has become so important (Huxhold 1991, 205). Depending on the equipment, one can accurately locate real or political boundaries or structures in two or three dimensions anywhere on earth. The advantage is that each

Figure 4.2   Three different projections of the continental United States demonstrate the possible variation. Image source: *Dana 1996.*

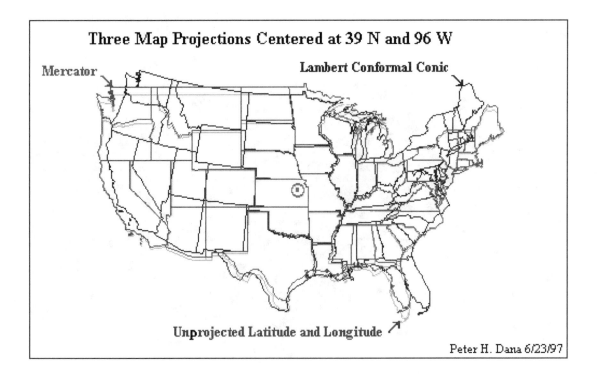

Three Map Projections Centered at 39 N and 96 W

Mercator

Lambert Conformal Conic

Unprojected Latitude and Longitude

Peter H. Dana 6/23/97

reading stands alone and is not dependent on another reading or on a series of surveys in order to reach a benchmark. The benefit of independent readings makes for much greater accuracy in base information. In the United States, GPS relies on 24 satellites circling the globe. As with much current technology, the equipment has improved dramatically in recent years. You can rely on surveyors, most of whom own and use GPS equipment these days, or you can take a course and learn its operation in three or four days.

Another advance in technology is the laser range finder. When used in combination with a GPS unit, a laser range finder is especially helpful in taking measurements without trespassing. The range finder can give horizontal and vertical measurements up to 1,500 feet away. It has internal software that calculates geometry and derives coordinates for any visible target. This technology eliminates the need to dance with the bull or his owner.

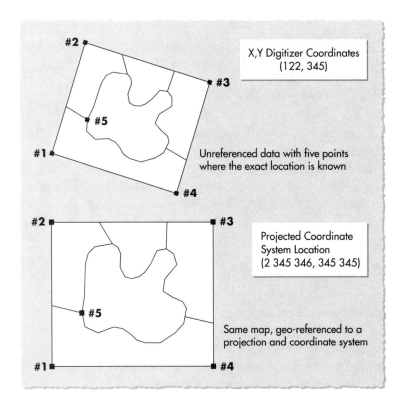

X,Y Digitizer Coordinates
(122, 345)

Unreferenced data with five points
where the exact location is known

Projected Coordinate
System Location
(2 345 346, 345 345)

Same map, geo-referenced to a
projection and coordinate system

Figure 4.3   Rectification is the task of adjusting newly digitized or imported data to a grid such as a State Plane coordinate system.

The major advantage of geo-referencing and rectification is the ability to accurately align data from many different sources. Thus, basic themes as well as analysis maps from various consultants can be successfully merged in a single image.

Rasters and Vectors

The two most common GIS formats are raster and vector. The raster format is like your television screen; small grids make up the images. In a raster GIS, grid cells represent conditions across the study area. The size of each grid cell can vary dramatically: some are as large as a mile on a side; others are as small as a meter on a side. This cell size is referred to as "resolution." The size will depend on the quality of the data you can acquire, the purpose of your study, the overall size of your files as compared with the size of your computer's storage capacity, and the data input method you plan to use. Obviously, for a given project, as the grid cell size gets smaller, the total number of cells gets exponentially larger. Often one must balance finer resolution with practical issues like computing speed and storage capacity. Some studies compromise with smaller, nested cells in the busy parts of the study area, such as the urbanized areas, and larger cells over the rural areas.

RASTERS HANDLE TRANSITIONS WELL

The advantage of the raster format is the ability to represent gradual changes clearly. For instance, vegetation types often transition from one community to another. Using the raster format, transition zones can be mapped as a continuously changing mixture of vegetation types. The following discussion on vector formats will show that natural transitions are not so gracefully accomplished in that format. In general, raster formats work well for natural systems and large study areas.

One disadvantage of raster maps is that only one condition is shown in each cell, usually the condition that fills the majority of the cell, although sometimes it is the condition nearest the cell centroid. If cells are relatively large, much data can be lost, especially comparatively small elements such as roads, power lines, mine entries, or springs. When there is a need for information to be more accurate at some point than at others, a combination of raster and vector formats is useful.

Figure 4.4 Global positioning system equipment has become more compact, more accurate, and easier to use.

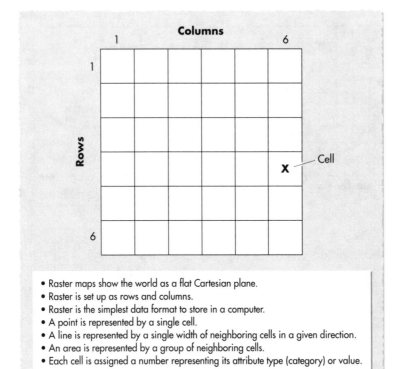

- Raster maps show the world as a flat Cartesian plane.
- Raster is set up as rows and columns.
- Raster is the simplest data format to store in a computer.
- A point is represented by a single cell.
- A line is represented by a single width of neighboring cells in a given direction.
- An area is represented by a group of neighboring cells.
- Each cell is assigned a number representing its attribute type (category) or value.

Figure 4.5   Raster data structure.

VECTORS ARE PRECISE

The vector format is tailor-made for urban systems. There are few transitions in urban areas. One block is zoned commercial; the next is zoned residential. There is no transitional area between them. Land use is usually described on a lot-by-lot basis, as is ownership type. One side of a line is private property; the other side is the city's right-of-way.

THE POINT IS . . .

In the vector format, every element is designated as a point, a line, or a polygon. Remember, there is no scale inside the GIS, so the point is simply a designation of *x* and *y* coordinates; it has no real size as far as the map is concerned. It can be shown on maps as a dot or as an icon.

LINES ARE WELL DEFINED

Every line in the vector format has two ends. If a line is curving or jagged, it will be divided into segments, with vertices or

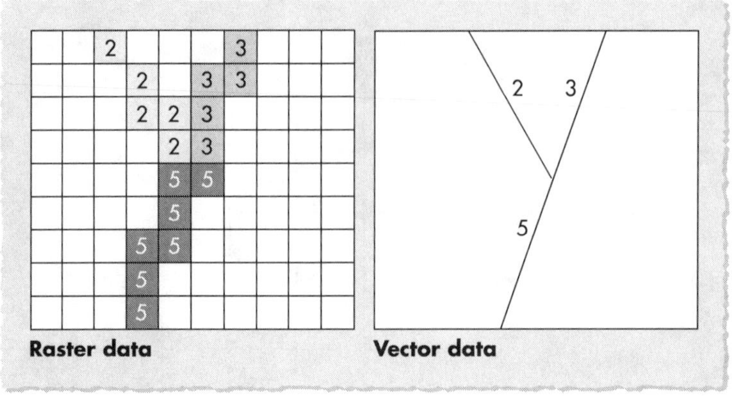

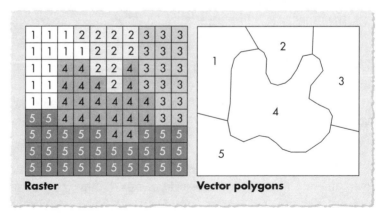

Figure 4.6 *Linear data representation in two GIS formats (raster and vector).*

shape points along its length. Each line segment has a length and a direction. Lines can be given many types of attributes. Pipelines have a purpose based on what they carry, they are made of a certain material, they have a given diameter, they were installed in a given year, and so on.

A roadway may be shown as a single line or as multiple, parallel lines to represent lanes. The attributes for roads can include their designated type (highway, major collector, residential street, alley, etc.), their surface material, whether they have curbs or ditches, their posted speed, and whether or not they are "one-way." These attributes take on special roles in network analysis where one task is to decide which route will be faster for emergency response vehicles.

Figure 4.7 *Raster data is easy to store when precision is not so critical. Vector data is much more precise but requires more labor, more computing power, and more computer storage.*

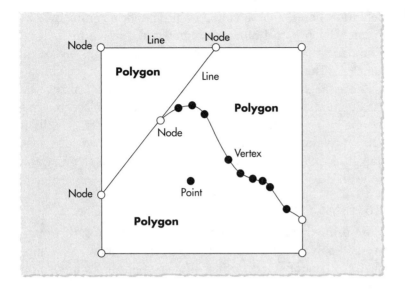

Figure 4.8   Vector data structure.

Where lines intersect, a node is created. These nodes can have their own attributes. Roadway intersections can have stop signs, stop lights, merge lanes, U-turns, and so forth. Some intersections will have non-nodes, such as a rail line on a separate grade from the road that passes beneath it. Once again, these non-nodes become important bits of information for network analysis and for AM/FM (automated mapping/facilities management) operations. AM/FM is used by public works departments, water districts, and utility companies to manage and maintain their infrastructures. The discussion that follows here and in Chapter 6 on topology expands on the functionality of lines and nodes in GIS.

RASTER AND VECTOR GIVE THE BEST OF BOTH WORLDS

Points and lines can be combined with raster data to take advantage of the efficiency of the raster format and still maintain the accuracy of the vector data. It works well to use the raster format in rural or natural areas and overlay certain elements, such as jurisdiction and property boundaries, roadways, utilities, and archeological sites (point data), as vectors.

POLYGONS HAVE INTRIGUING NATURES

Most of the difficulties in vector formats arise from polygons. A polygon is used to outline a two-dimensional area such as a detention pond, a flood zone, a soil type, or a zoning overlay district. Each parcel of land is a polygon defined by its legal boundary. A problem can arise when the ends of the polygon do not close. The GIS does not read it as a polygon and can not calculate an enclosed area when you ask for reports. Usually you can zoom in on the end points to make sure they close, but this is time-consuming. Most sophisticated GIS packages will let you set tolerances, within which they will automatically close polygons for you, once you have designated an element as a polygon.

SLIVERS ARE A NUISANCE

More difficult problems relate to the coincidence of similar, overlaid polygons. For instance, if property boundaries are supplied by a county clerk's office, they may not fit accurately on

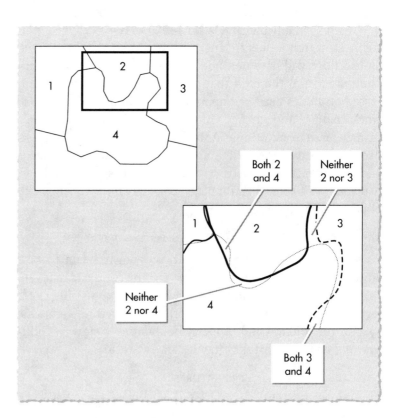

Figure 4.9   Slivers result when polygons on overlaid themes do not coincide with each other.

the city's streets and rights-of-way boundaries. There are likely to be overlapping areas where the property lines do not quite line up with the right-of-way lines. When these themes are combined, the GIS will read all the resultant shapes as new polygons. These small overlapping areas are called "slivers," and they make life very interesting for GIS technicians all over the country.

MCHARGIAN SLIVERS CAUSE MAJOR PROBLEMS

A real nuisance is slivers in the natural domain. When McHargian suitability overlays are being done, values are assigned to certain conditions and the sum of those values will lead the planner or designer to make certain recommendations. Consider, however, that certain values have been assigned to each vegetation type and other values to each of the soil types. Often vegetation types coincide with soil types. But if the polygons do not line up accurately, and they seldom do from one natural theme to the next, sums will be derived that are misleading or meaningless. The intersection of the misaligned polygons will result in slivers, sometimes hundreds of them, and the summed values will not give the results for which the model was designed. Again, tolerances can be applied to eliminate the smallest slivers, but the larger ones have to be reviewed one at a time.

TOPOLOGY IS DEFINED

The major advantage of vector formats is that all that recording of lines and nodes allows the GIS to generate a topologic structure. Here is an example of topology. Within a city, the centerline of each street has a node at each intersection. A line segment between nodes represents one block, and that line segment has a direction corresponding to the increase in address numbers moving up the block. In addition, topology includes a precise location of the element relative to the study's grid system. The line segment is noted in the database, as well as each node. Attributes can be attached to the line segment and to the nodes. For the line segment these attributes may include pavement type, whether the street includes parking or bike lanes, whether it is one-way or a part of a bus route. Data attached to the nodes may include whether there is a traffic light, stop signs, or crosswalks, or the number of recent accidents at that corner.

Topology not only describes precise locations of the elements, but also describes the relationship of points, lines, and polygons to one another. A point may reside on a line or within a polygon. A line may be on the edge of a polygon or partially within it. Topology identifies the image element (line, point, polygon) with a key in the database that accompanies the GIS maps, and it gives the database more functionality. Some analytical operators require topology to function. These will be described in Chapter 6.

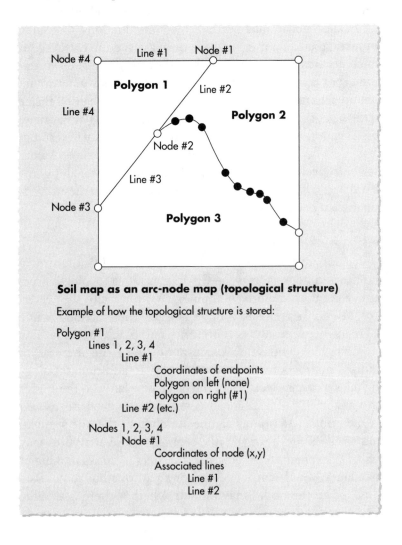

Figure 4.10   Topological structure of linework within a GIS.

As we can see, there are advantages and disadvantages to raster and vector formats. Software packages are available for either, and some include both. Scanned input lends itself more readily to the raster format, whereas the vector format usually requires digitized input. There are no hard-and-fast rules, but in general, raster files are common for natural areas, and vector files are almost all that will be found for urban areas. Some people use vector formats exclusively.

GIS MAPS ARE NOT TO SCALE

Notice in the foregoing discussion that the concept of scale was not mentioned. There really is no scale in the GIS, except those which are temporarily assigned for viewing the images on the monitor or for printing hard copies. Consequently, it is always a good idea to include a bar scale with each image so that, as the image size changes, the designer will have an idea of the scale.

Relational Databases

Most GIS packages come with their own databases, and these are populated as the data is input. Because there are other very important existing databases, such as the census data, it is often desirable to link the GIS to another database outside the system. As software is upgraded, this linkage is becoming an easier feat than it once was.

Currently, most internal GIS databases and most commercially available databases and Database Management System (DBMS) software is relational in format. In relational databases the data is stored in rows and columns, in separate tables of related data. There can be many tables, each with rows and columns, and within each table is a column known as a key. The key is used to relate the data to their locations on the maps. Thus, the tables can be joined or separated, or pieces of the data can be selected and manipulated (Huxhold 1991). Bits of information in the tables are called records. Another important feature of modern, robust databases is that the files are separated from the programs. This separation allows much greater flexibility (ibid., 9).

Because so many people are now using them, DBMSs use programs based on high-level languages. High-level languages are much more user friendly than lower-level, but require more power and storage room within the computer. The lower in the hierarchy a language is, the longer the instructions will be for a particular task; generally that language will be more difficult to learn, and thus there are fewer persons who are available to write low-level programs. High-level programs are based on a syntax such as Structured Query Language (SQL) or Query by Example (QBE) (Date 1983, 33).

The difference between SQL and QBE is that SQL is attractive to "people who are used to thinking in a verbal or word-oriented manner" and QBE appeals to "people who are more comfortable with a visual or picture-oriented manner of thinking." In SQL, commands are given with stylized sentences, but "the user in QBE operates by filling in blanks in empty tables on the screen" (Date 1983, 101). It's probably safe to say that most designers and planners would be more comfortable with the QBE format, if they dare get that close to DBMS in the first place. Remember, DBMSs are very widespread, and there are lots of consultants and freelancers willing to work on more sophisticated GIS projects.

GIS Analytical Operators

GIS analytical operators support map-based algebra and are used to manipulate the data. They are the engines that perform the tasks assigned for analysis. Analytical operators can add values shown on overlaid themes; they can accumulate value while moving across the surface of a theme; they can define buffers around features such as roads or schools or airports; they can identify clusters and their centroids. In his book, *Geographic Systems and Cartographic Modeling,* C. Dana Tomlin (1990) describes more than four dozen operators possible in a GIS. Some of these come as standard features in most GISs, and some require additional programming in order to facilitate their use. Most GIS packages are designed to allow for the use of a fairly standard command language to employ new operators. See Chapter 6 for more details.

Computer Models

A computer model is a sequence of instructions designed to yield maps and/or quantitative data that will facilitate decision making. Chapter 6 explores the workings of the current models used in land planning and site design. Chapter 10 describes a new, "graphic" model developed by the author specifically for site design.

SUGGESTED READING

A number of excellent books have been published in recent years covering the basics of GIS, as well as its applications. Here are some of the standard texts along with some of the more popular works.

Antenucci, John C., et al. *Geographic Information Systems: A Guide to the Technology.* New York: Van Nostrand Reinhold, 1991. Probably the most complete, up-to-date, practical guide to the use of GIS this book is written for GIS users and is fairly easy to understand.

Berry, Joseph. *Beyond Mapping.* Ft. Collins, CO: GIS World, Inc., 1993. This is a compilation of Mr. Berry's highly successful monthly columns in *GIS World.* He is the philosopher of GIS, looking at issues from many perspectives; whenever possible he does so in a humorous manner.

Burrough, Peter A. *Principles of Geographical Information Systems for Land Resources Assessment.* New York: Oxford University Press, 1986. Here is a "how-to" for serious GIS users. It focuses on the step-by-step procedures needed to set up and operate a GIS.

Davis, Bruce. *GIS: A Visual Approach.* Santa Fe, NM: Onword Press, 1996. An illustrated version of "GIS for Dummies." There are lots of images representing GIS concepts and operations. This book makes a good GIS reference, especially for beginners.

Huxhold, William E. *An Introduction to Urban Geographic Information Systems.* New York: Oxford University Press, 1991. This work is both conceptual and empirical. It discusses the theories behind GIS and describes several examples of municipalities and counties that have used GIS for a variety of solutions.

Star, Jeffrey, and John Estes. *Geographic Information Systems: An Introduction.* Englewood Cliffs, NJ: Prentice-Hall, 1990. A primer on the terminology and basic concepts of GIS. This work is thorough and well illustrated.

Tomlin, C. Dana. *Geographic Information Systems and Cartographic Modeling.* Englewood Cliffs, NJ: Prentice-Hall, 1990. An advanced look at most of the analytical operators available in today's GIS software. This book is thorough and precise, and not recommended for beginners.

A number of other compendiums and compilations exist. GIS is used by many different disciplines; a review of the literature will take you from archaeology to building maintenance, chemical pollution, dendrochronology, emergency routing, and on and on.

REFERENCES

Antenucci, John C., Kay Brown, Peter L. Croswell, and Michael J. Kevany. 1991. *Geographic Information Systems: A Guide to the Technology.* New York: Van Nostrand Reinhold.

Berry, Joseph K. 1993. *Beyond Mapping, Concepts, Algorithms and Issues in GIS.* Fort Collins, CO: GIS World, Inc.

Burrough, Peter A. 1986. *Principles of Geographical Information Systems for Land Resources Assessment.* Oxford: Oxford University Press.

Dana, Peter H. 1996. *The Geographer's Craft* (web page). Austin: University of Texas. URL: www.utexas.edu/depts/grg/gcraft/ notes/gps/gps.html

Date, C. J. 1983. *Database: A Primer.* Menlo Park, CA: Addison-Wesley.

Davis, Bruce E. 1991. *GIS: A Visual Approach.* Santa Fe, NM: Onword Press.

Huxhold, William E. 1991. *An Introduction to Urban Geographic Information Systems.* New York: Oxford University Press.

Star, Jeffrey, and John Estes. 1990. *Geographic Information Systems: An Introduction.* Englewood Cliffs, NJ: Prentice-Hall.

Tomlin, C. Dana. 1990. *Geographic Information Systems and Cartographic Modeling.* Englewood Cliffs, NJ: Prentice-Hall.

5

Where Does the Data Come From?

TRADITIONAL COLLECTION METHODS

We know we cannot begin a project without information. Typically, information about property lines, contours, drainages and
water bodies, existing structures, utilities, and so on, is collected by the civil engineer or surveyor who has been hired by
the client. This person either collects the data in the field, gets it
from the municipal or county clerk, or, more recently, down-
loads it from the Internet. The landscape architect may go to the
site to prepare an inventory of trees, major shrubs, native plant
communities, views, landforms, major rock outcrops, potential
access points, and so forth. A biologist may inspect the site to
search for rare plants or to identify plant communities. Political
information, such as jurisdictions, land use, and ownership,
comes from the county clerk or the local planning department.
Many more types of information may be needed in order to analyze and make recommendations for development and/or management of a site, but when sites are small, this information
gathering is not an overwhelming task.

NO IN-THE-FIELD DATA COLLECTION HERE

When sites are large, remote, or otherwise inaccessible, data
collection can become a daunting task. One must rely on the
data of others. Most GIS projects include site visits, but these
visits are not so much for detailed information gathering as for a
general survey of the study area and the context in which it sits.

Usually some team members will return to do field checks of digital data to verify accuracy, currency, and resolution. Site visits are also helpful once recommendations have been suggested and the planners and designers want to do a "common sense" check before going public with their findings.

THE DATA OF OTHERS

Who supplies data? Lots of people do. The United States is data-rich as compared with many other nations, as is Canada, which started nationwide data collection long before the United States (Antenucci 1991, 21). Many U.S. government agencies collect, organize, and distribute data free or for a nominal fee. Much of this data is further refined by value-added resellers (VARs), who check for accuracy and add labels and database connections. Data exist for the entire United States. The data sets are not uniformly complete nor are all of high quality, but some data exist for every square mile of this country.

Federal Collectors

Within the Office of Management and Budget (OMB) is the Federal Geographic Data Committee (FGDC), whose task it is to set standards and coordinate data collection and dispersal among all the federal agencies. The FGDC maintains a comprehensive list of federal, state, and local data on its website at:

http://www.fgdc.gov

For more than a decade the National Mapping Division (NMD) of the U.S. Geological Survey (USGS) has been collecting data for its National Digital Cartographic Data Base (NDCDB). The two major products of this database are digital elevation models (DEMs) and digital line graphs (DLGs), both of which are described in the chart on page 54. The National Interagency Mapping Agency (NIMA) of the Department of Defense collects and processes aerial photography and remotely sensed (satellite) data in great quantities.

Statewide Coverages

Most states maintain complete GIS coverages for their highways, waterways, forests, and state-managed wildlife areas and recreation areas. Of these, the highway departments' are usually the most sophisticated. Theirs may include data for surface types, maintenance records, traffic loads, accidents, jurisdictions, rights-of-way, and intersecting easements. Many state highway departments maintain fairly current aerial photography of all their roads. However, not all of this data is available to the public.

Homegrown Data

Local data suppliers such as municipalities, counties, agencies and consortia are becoming much more effective in updating their files and providing information in a variety of formats. Several states encourage data control at the local level. Local agency staff are better able to verify data accuracy, because they live and work in the geographic region covered by the data, and they have greater incentives to keep the data accurate.

Figure 5.1 *Recent aerial photos provide good information on streets, trees, and land use.*

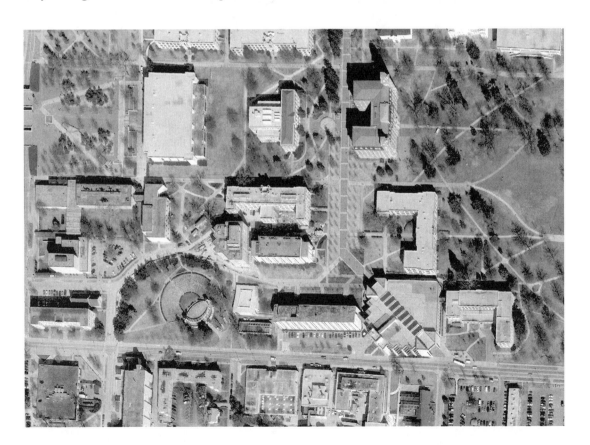

Commercial Off-the-Shelf Data

Commercial vendors are providing user-specific data in regular releases. Many of their customers are involved in locating retail stores, fast-food franchises, gas/convenience stores, and entertainment facilities. Their data foci are primarily demographics and traffic patterns.

QUALITY CONTROL

Metadata is information about the data itself: resolution, platform, available exchange file formats, currency, and coverages. Think of metadata as specifications for the information that planners or designers want to acquire. Much recent attention has been paid to increasing the availability and standardization of metadata. In some cases data can be very expensive, and metadata informs the purchaser about the content, form, and quality of the product before the purchase.

SUPPLIER/PRODUCT NAME	METADATA (BRIEF)
U.S. Geological Survey	
Quad Maps (paper)	Contours, roads, rivers, lakes, ponds, some structures, forests, political boundaries
	15° quads at a scale of 1:62500
	7.5° quads at a scale of 1:24000
Digital Line Graphs (DLGs)	Roads, rivers, shorelines, political boundaries
	Coverage for entire United States
	Derived from 1: 100,000 maps
Digital Elevation Models (DEMs)	Contours, spot heights (in grid cells)
	Coverage for entire United States
	Level one (hand processed); Level two (machine processed)
	Derived from 1: 24,000 quads
Digital Raster Graphics (DRGs)	Scanned from orthophoto quads at 1:24,000; 1:100,000
Defense Mapping Agency	Contours
Digital Terrain Models	Derived from 1:100,000 maps

SUPPLIER/PRODUCT NAME	METADATA (BRIEF)
National Resource Conservation Service (NRCS), formerly Soil Conservation Service	Soils (STATSCO). Maps and reports available by county
Biological Resources Service (BRS)	Wildlife habitats (based on State GAP projects). When files exist, coverages are statewide.
U.S. Forest Service	Timber stand maps; classification, resolution.
	Coverages vary with each forest.
Bureau of the Census	Demographic data (STF*)
	Roads, political boundaries (TIGER**).
	Generally, the USGS DLGs are more complete.
Environmental Protection Agency (EPA)	Reach files: stream topology, flows

* STF = Summary Tape File
** TIGER = Topologically Integrated Geographically Encoded and Referenced

TREND: LOCAL DATA COLLECTION

The current trend is toward local collection and management of data files, for several reasons. A few places have initiated fund-

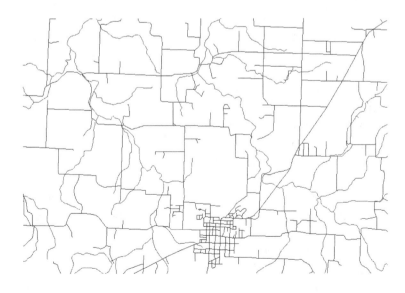

Figure 5.2   EPA provides streams information in vector format.

ing mechanisms that support data acquisition and management. Usually, the initial funding act is statewide and funds are distributed based on population or other formulae. It is the democratic approach to spend this money where it is collected and to collect it where the most benefit will accrue. If a county is experiencing tremendous growth, one way to protect the existing quality of life is with planning studies, especially those that include economic projections. Unless data is available, planning studies can be prohibitively expensive. The initial funding mechanism can be viewed as a protection tax.

Moreover, it is in the best interest of local people that their data is highly accurate, at a meaningful level of resolution, easy to interpret, and current. When large agencies such as federal or state governments take on data management, there is less incentive to do a good job everywhere. As budgets decline or funds are shifted within these agencies, the ability to provide uniformly dependable data also declines. It makes sense to develop and maintain data at the local level. The trend toward local data management is most prevalent in the Northeast and along the Atlantic seaboard; it is not yet as prevalent in the West and the South.

WHERE IS THE GOOD DATA?

The northeastern and Midatlantic states of Maine, Vermont, New Hampshire, Rhode Island, New York, and Massachusetts have data files for their entire jurisdictions. The state of New York has parcel boundaries and centroids for every parcel in the entire state. Some states, such as Vermont, New York, and Massachusetts, have the data decentralized so that it can be distributed and updated by regional planning commissions or other affiliates.

Vermont distributes its data through 12 regional planning commissions, each of which includes several counties and at least one large town. The regional planning commissions authorize planning studies to be done by town governments or outside consultants. The selectmen in each town review and debate the planning study's recommendations before enacting new policies.

Another data-rich state is Wisconsin. As a result of legislation in the late 1980s, the Wisconsin Land Information Program

(WLIP) allocates land transfer taxes to fund mapping and planning at the county level. All 72 Wisconsin counties have received funding to prepare their own databases, and they have all applied for and received additional grants for planning efforts. According to Georgia Hopf, grants coordinator for the WLIP Board, the availability of data and planning funds has also excited the imaginations of local citizens, who are more involved than ever in planning efforts. County mapping projects include wetlands mapping, establishment of geodetic control, and land records modernization. Planning projects include land use and zoning studies.

Other states that have initiated statewide mapping programs at the county level include Kansas, Virginia, and North Carolina. Additional data-rich states with active local planning groups are Massachusetts, Pennsylvania, Florida, Montana, Oregon, and California. States that use GIS on a regular basis within their own agencies include Alaska, Minnesota, Illinois,

Figure 5.3   Some states share data statewide, whereas others encourage the counties to maintain the databases.

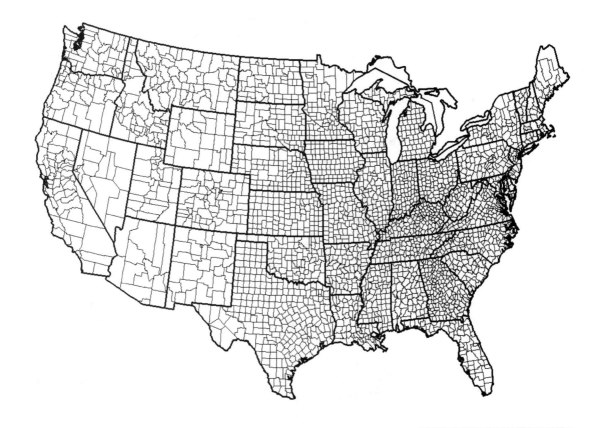

Wisconsin, Texas, and Maryland. Alaska, Iowa, Kentucky, and Oregon were among the first to enact legislation regulating public access to GIS databases (Antenucci 1991, 246). Everyone, from the director of the public works department to the head of the local grass roots organization, realizes the significance of a digital database, especially one that's part of a GIS.

All states have data, but their files may have one or more of the following shortcomings:

- The coverage is not yet complete for the entire state; thus, a particular study area may not be included.
- The resolution is too coarse for the need.
- If strong metadata standards are not in place, the accuracy and currency of the data may be unknown or below standard.
- The data is available only from a vendor, which means it may be quite expensive.

To locate available data in your state, contact the Federal Geographic Data Committee on the world wide web at www.fgdc.gov or by writing to FGDC, 590 National Center, Reston, VA 20192 (Hoch 1995). If you have to contract for data collection, make sure you get a licensing agreement and check the metadata up front (Olsenholler 1997).

SUSPICIOUS DATA

One of the most irritating situations occurs when you are not sure your data is accurate. When accurate data at an appropriate resolution is available, all is well. When data is not available or contains inconsistencies, it becomes very difficult to use. Once you know your data is flawed, you lose confidence in that data and, perhaps, in the project itself.

REFERENCES

Antenucci, John C., Kay Brown, Peter L. Croswell, Michael J. Kevany, and Hugh Archer. 1991. *Geographic Information Systems: A Guide to the Technology.* New York: Van Nostrand Reinhold.

Hoch, Robert B. 1995. "Federal Geographic Data Committee Reaches a Crossroads." *GIS World* (Fort Collins, CO), Sept.

Olsenholler, Jeff. 1997. "Find the Right Fit: How to Select the Best Data Collection Strategy." *GIS World* (Fort Collins, CO), July.

SUGGESTED READING

In 1990, the Mapping Science Committee of the National Research Council published *Spatial Data Needs: The Future of the National Mapping Program,* and in 1991 it released *Research and Development in the National Mapping Division, USGS: Trends and Prospects.* Both of these reports established guidelines for the continued collection and processing of federal data. The National Research Council produced a report in 1993, *Toward a Coordinated Spatial Data Infrastructure for the Nation,* which identified the major issues relevant to data collection, listed the federal agencies that had been designated to collect each type of data, and evaluated the current state of the National Spatial Data Infrastructure (NSDI).

What Makes It Magic: A Brief Introduction to Operators and Models

Imagine that you have put data in your GIS, so you have a database and you have maps. Each map shows a data theme: soils, vegetation, or ownership, for example. You have viewed each map on your monitor and printed it out, so you know the data has been entered correctly. You have completed some sample queries on your database and checked to make sure the reports are accurate. Everything is ready; now what do you do?

Some firms and agencies just print maps and issue inventory reports. This is a primitive use of the tool. Essentially, they use their GIS as a retrieval system. Information retrieval is the mandate of distribution agencies and some municipal departments. Some GIS consulting firms do this as well. There is a lot of software that supports these simple GIS actions, and most of it is quite reasonably priced. Basic, map-making packages are simple tools for simple products.

However, GISs are sophisticated tools. Design professionals do not earn their living by printing maps and making copies of their databases. For them, the data must be fuel to the fires of analysis and synthesis. The spark that ignites the fire is the GIS analytical operator. What is an analytical operator? It can be an algorithm, a mathematic manipulator, a data converter, a number cruncher; it's any tool that allows professionals to act on the data. Attributes are the types of data within a given theme. In the world of manual analysis, attributes are called categories. In the vegetation theme, two attributes may be oak woodlands and tall grass prairie. One operator, called "reclass" (or "recode"), will allow a person to assign values to each attribute. If he or she then assigns values to the vegetation theme and the soils theme, another operator, "sum," will allow the person to add the value of each vegetation attribute to the value of each soils attribute on a cell-by-cell (or polygon-by-polygon) basis. Professional expertise is needed in deciding what values to assign.

With professional direction, the right analytical operators will transform the data into conclusions and recommendations. This book does not explore the internal structure of these operators, because there are many good publications that already do that; several are listed at the end of Chapter 4. Instead, this discussion focuses on how a designer may use these tools.

HOUSEKEEPING OPERATORS

There are some operators in GIS that are used for basic data entry and modification. These include map coordinate translation, map projection transformation, rubber sheeting, edge matching, raster/vector conversion, map merging and extraction. These are important tools, but they do not enhance analysis so much as they improve or complete basic thematic maps. They are fully explained in the software manuals and most training programs. If you work with a GIS technician, you need only know that they exist, and that when themes don't line up, the base maps may need adjusting with one of these operators.

ANALYTICAL OPERATORS OVERVIEW

The analytical and predictive operators can be grouped in several ways; this discussion classifies GIS operators by their function. These classifications include terrain analysis, network analysis, overlay, database-initiated analysis, map algebra, address matching, and distance/direction operators. The following chart shows examples of operators by functional classification. Of the references listed in Chapter 4, John Antenucci's book gives clear definitions of the operators discussed here and several more, and Bruce Davis's book uses illustrations and examples to define most of these operators and many more.

Overview of GIS Operators

CLASSIFICATION	EXAMPLE OPERATORS
Terrain analysis	Generate contours; generate aspect; generate slope; generate drainages; generate elevation; calculate viewsheds
Overlay*	Intersect areas from two themes and create new combined zones; overlay vectors on rasters; identify features from one layer within polygons from another (visual integrity, for instance); apply a mask of one theme to another; recolor
Map algebra*	Reclass values, sum assigned values within polygons of combined themes; select maximum (or minimum) value of overlaid themes; weight value of one theme relative to another and produce sum in each polygon; use value of one theme as multiplier of values in second theme; use matrix to reassign values and use mathematical operator
Distance/direction	Create buffers; make linear measurements, perimeter measurements, area measurements; do a radius search; prepare cost surface accumulations; gravitate across elevation surface
Database-initiated analysis	Recode according to matrix; generate coincidence tables
Address matching	Assign address ranges per street segment; locate addresses from list on map
Network analysis	Determine routes: fastest, least distance; reach all addresses; balance multiple routes

* In this chart, *overlay* refers to graphic overlay, whereas mathematical overlays fall within the classification of map algebra.

COMMONLY USED OPERATORS IN LAND PLANNING

Not all of the operators listed in the chart are used frequently by land planners and site designers, so this chapter focuses on those that are most commonly used. Not only are the basic functions described, but for those persons who have not used a GIS before, tips are given and pitfalls are identified. The GIS operators most frequently used by land planners and site designers are:

- All the terrain analysis operators, including slope and viewshed
- Overlay (combined themes), including vectors over rasters, visual integrity analysis, and recolor
- Map algebra, including sum and reclass (or recode)
- Distance/direction, including area measurement, line measurement, and buffers

Terrain Analysis Operators

We begin from the ground up. One of my professors once said that "grading and drainage is the bread and butter of landscape architecture." At the time I thought he meant that a sizable portion of the fees came from that type of work. Later I realized he meant that a large proportion of our site decisions are based on topography, and we have to know what is happening with the grades in order to be effective designers. This topographic dominance is equally true when one works in a GIS.

The preceding chart shows that terrain analysis operators can be used to generate contours, elevation, aspect, slope, and drainages. We will look at viewsheds separately, followed by visual integrity.

Elevation Maps

Although elevation is used more in the analysis of relatively large study areas than for small sites, don't dismiss the use of elevation maps. If a study area includes dramatic elevation changes, they can point to differences in plant communities, microclimates, wildlife habitat, or heating and cooling days for a development. In some special plant communities, changes of a few feet (sometimes even inches) can mean differences in native species.

In GIS an elevation map can be useful in selecting viewing points from which to calculate viewsheds. Depending on the contour interval, the elevation map may have no more information than a contour map, but the spaces between the contours are colored (or shaded) and show a progression from high to low, making the map very easy to read. If the contours have been generalized, the elevation map may show more detail than the associated contour map. Because it is so easy to generate, the elevation theme is a handy map to use when selecting viewing locations and is sometimes used for broad planting design decisions.

GIS Contours

Contours are lines of equal elevation, usually expressed in whole numbers and at a variety of contour intervals. These can be entered as such, or derived from spot heights. Digital line graphs (DLGs) generated from 1:100,000-scale maps from the USGS provide contours as part of the data set, but DLGs are not as detailed as the information derived from digital elevation models (DEMs) generated from 1:24,000-scale quadrangle maps, also from the USGS. DEMs provide raster elevation, from which contours can be plotted by the GIS. Obviously, the denser the spot heights, or in this case the elevation grid cells, the more accurate the contours will be.

The computer will ask for the contour interval before it begins to plot contours. You will not have to interpolate; you

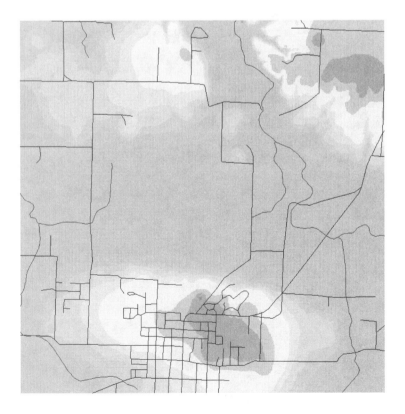

Figure 6.1 *A digital elevation model is supplied by USGS in a raster format.*

can let the computer do it. Unlike what happens with hand interpolation, if the resultant map is too busy because the interval is too small, it only takes a few seconds to select another interval and wait for another set of contours to appear. The computer will also give more contours when a smaller interval is selected. Do not think that a smaller interval will improve the accuracy of the data; the computer is still performing its interpolating algorithms based on the initial DEM data. The computer can generalize, but it cannot improve on the quality of the basic data. Interpolation is actually a computer model, because it involves a number of steps (Burrough 1986). It is almost universal in GIS software, and most people have come to think of it as an operator.

Aspect

Aspect shows the direction a slope faces: north, east, south, west, or any direction in between. Flat areas (as defined by the

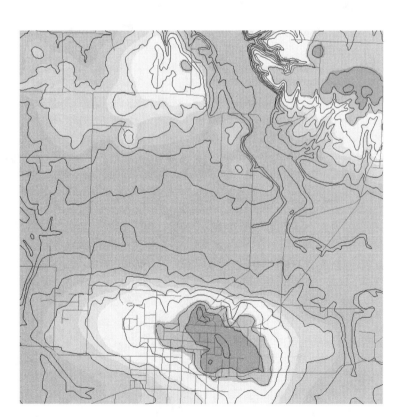

Figure 6.2 *The raster elevation data is used to interpolate contours. This is a digital elevation model (DEM) with contour lines and county roads overlaid.*

user) have "no aspect." The designer's role in making the selection of aspect categories is to decide how the information will be used. How many degrees of aspect are meaningful in evaluating existing site conditions?

If you are planning to take your analysis from GIS into CADD for construction documents, you might think about

Figure 6.3   A computer-generated aspect map showing degrees from North. Zero (0) values indicate flat areas; the shading divides the slopes into six aspect directions of 60 degrees each.

108	90	117	117	90	108	135	135	108	90	117	117	90	108	135	135	108	90	90	90	90	90	90	90	90	90	90	90	90	90
117	90	108	135	0	135	108	117	117	90	108	135	108	90	90	117	117	90	90	90	90	90	90	90	90	90	90	90	90	90
135	0	135	108	90	117	117	108	135	135	108	117	117	90	90	108	135	108	90	90	90	90	90	90	90	90	90	90	90	90
108	90	117	117	90	108	135	108	90	117	117	117	117	90	90	90	117	117	90	90	90	90	90	90	90	90	90	90	90	90
117	90	108	135	135	108	117	117	90	108	135	135	117	90	90	90	108	135	108	90	90	90	90	90	90	90	90	90	90	90
135	0	135	108	117	117	108	135	135	108	117	135	135	108	90	90	90	117	117	90	90	90	90	90	90	90	90	90	90	90
135	108	117	117	108	135	135	108	117	117	108	135	135	117	90	90	90	117	117	90	90	90	90	90	90	90	90	90	90	90
117	117	108	135	135	108	117	117	108	135	108	117	135	135	108	90	90	117	121	98	90	90	90	90	90	90	90	90	90	90
108	135	135	108	117	117	108	135	108	117	117	117	117	117	101	98	98	121	121	98	90	90	90	90	90	90	90	90	90	90
0	135	135	117	108	135	108	117	117	117	117	121	108	101	121	113	90	98	121	121	98	90	90	90	90	90				
135	135	135	135	135	135	117	117	117	117	117	117	135	121	98	113	124	98	90	98	121	121	98	90	90	90	82			
117	135	135	135	135	135	135	135	117	117	117	117	135	135	121	108	124	113	90	90	98	121	121	98	90	90	67			
108	135	135	135	135	135	135	135	135	121	108	124	124	124	117	117	117	90	90	90	98	121	121	90	79	59				
0	135	135	135	135	135	135	135	135	135	121	124	124	124	124	124	124	98	90	90	90	98	121	90	63	79				
135	135	135	135	135	135	135	135	135	135	135	135	135	135	135	135	121	121	98	90	90	90	98	90	82	82				
117	135	135	135	135	135	135	135	135	135	135	135	135	135	108	121	121	98	90	90	90	90	79	59						
108	135	135	135	135	135	135	135	135	135	135	135	135	135	135	121	108	124	113	90	90	90	82	59	59					
108	117	135	117	117	135	135	135	135	135	135	135	135	135	124	124	113	113	124	98	90	82	59	59	72					
117	117	135	117	117	135	135	135	135	153	153	153	149	146	146	146	135	126	117	98	121	117	90	63	59	72	59			
135	135	135	135	135	135	135	135	135	153	153	149	146	146	146	146	144	135	124	98	98	101	90	79	82	67	56			
117	135	117	117	135	135	135	135	135	135	146	146	146	144	135	144	146	135	117	101	98	90	82	79	59	56				
117	135	117	117	135	135	135	135	135	135	146	146	153	146	146	146	135	117	117	117	90	63	45	45	27					
135	135	135	135	135	135	135	135	135	135	146	146	146	153	144	135	135	135	117	108	135	0	45	27	18	18				
135	135	135	135	135	135	135	135	135	135	146	146	146	153	153	149	153	153	135	0	0	0	0	360	360	45				
117	117	135	117	117	135	135	135	153	149	135	146	146	146	157	172	180	180	180	0	0	0	0	0	360	360	0			
135	117	135	117	117	135	135	135	153	162	149	149	162	157	149	169	180	180	180	0	0	0	0	0	360	360	0			
153	135	135	135	135	135	135	135	135	149	162	149	149	172	180	180	180	198	207	225	0	0	0	0	360	360	0			
135	135	117	117	135	135	162	153	153	153	169	172	153	169	169	153	162	225	225	225	225	0	0	0	360	360	0			
135	153	135	108	135	0	180	180	180	169	153	172	169	153	162	153	135	0	225	207	198	0	0	0	360	360	0			

redoing the aspect analysis before the export. This adjustment makes the categories meaningful in construction terms, which may be different from the original analysis needs. Once in CADD, the aspect zones can be used to specify hydroseed mixes or for plant selection or for deciding which slopes will get irrigation and which will not. Both GIS and CADD can take measurements and generate reports. Both can tell how many square feet or how many acres exist at each aspect. This type of information is very useful for cost estimating.

Slope

Slope equals rise over run. Slope is the angle at which land surfaces sit, usually expressed as a percentage or as a ratio of vertical rise to horizontal distance. It is important to define meaningful slope categories; one can always tell when a nondesigner sets the slope categories. A common nondesigner set is 0 to 25%, 26% to 50%, and so forth. These categories (or attribute types) may have meaning for wildlife habitat, but they are not very useful for

Figure 6.4 Computer-generated slope map with banding along the contour lines in flat areas. This is due to the raster cell size and the minimum elevation change allowed between adjacent cells. In this case, the minimum elevation change is 1 meter and the raster cell resolution is 10 meters.

development or construction decisions. For site designers a more meaningful set might be 0 to 2%, 3 to 5%, 6 to 10%, 11 to 25%, and anything over 25%. Most GIS programs will prompt the designer for the categories as part of the operating sequence. Again, the GIS can tell you how much land falls in each slope category. Use this slope report when fine-tuning the proposed program of uses and the amounts of related features.

One precaution, as with all GIS output, is to make a common sense check. Occasionally, the computer will see things in a distorted way. We have seen slope maps that have bands of color and white. When the data were queried, the colored areas had an assigned slope and the white areas had "no data." Of course, data were input in those areas. Checking the algorithm, we learned that there was a problem between the grid cell size and the contour interval. Do not let this or other minor problems deter you from using GIS. Anomalies such as this one can be overcome, but only if you recognize that there is problem in

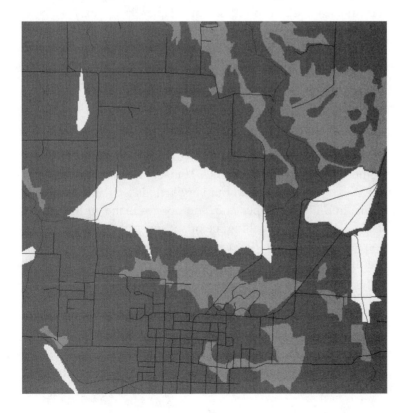

Figure 6.5 A corrected slope map becomes one of the overlaid themes in a computer model.

the first place. Just because the computer does the work, it doesn't mean we should stop questioning the results.

Another consideration when going from the GIS environment into the CADD environment is that the existing GIS slope polygons can be imported to form the basis for feature siting. The site analysis method shown in Chapter 10 includes slope as a theme. Its prominence in the resulting site analysis is based on its ranking among the included themes. However, the slope theme is always available to be placed as an overlay on the site analysis in doing further analysis, whether in GIS or in CADD.

Rivers and Streams

Major drainages such as rivers and streams are part of the base data that is either digitized from paper maps, imported from the DLGs, or from the EPA's "reach files." Occasionally they come from another source, such as a database generated by a state's department of natural resources or a water control board.

Reach files have the added advantage of including topology and drainage data. As discussed in Chapter 4, topology refers to the identification of each image segment. Topology identifies the segment's georeferenced location and ties it to any number of attributes in the database. Reach files note stream gauging stations, peak flows, average flows, confluences, headwaters, bridges, and dams.

Flooding

Flood data is not as prevalent in digital form as many other data themes. The Federal Emergency Management Agency (FEMA) provides some flood data, but very little is available in digital format and FEMA's paper maps do not cover the entire United States. If the client is willing, he or she will hire hydrology engineers to calculate the flood areas, based on a given frequency, and hiring a professional engineer is standard practice for most major GIS studies. Some counties in the West have flood control divisions within their engineering or public works departments, but not many do and they may not share their data.

CREATIVE DATA GENERATION

Sometimes flood data is not available and the project does not warrant the expense of another consultant. Other sources to consider are the Sanborn insurance maps and the soils maps from the National Resource Conservation Service (NRCS). Many soils reports identify types that are "frequently flooded." This data interpretation is not a very scientific approach, and the soils data will not tell you the difference between a 10-year flood and a 100-year event, but sometimes a map of this type is all that can be developed. If your study area is large, the computer can select these soil types for you with a "reclass" operation, as described in a later section, "Reclass and Recolor."

If the study area is small, you can often interview city maintenance or emergency crews. Take them to the field along with base maps and mark the high-water lines based on their testimony. The maps can then be digitized.

In urban areas the Sanborn maps often note flood hazard, and these insurance maps are available at most local libraries. As with the soils derivation, neither city crews nor the Sanborn

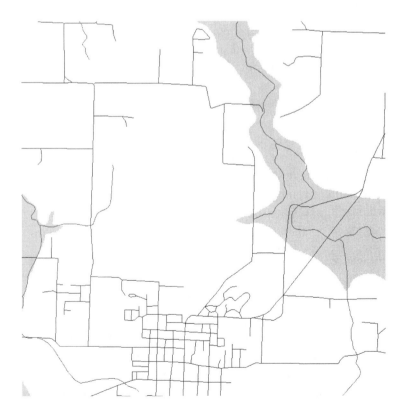

Figure 6.6   Floodplain theme obtained from FEMA.

maps will decipher the exact magnitude of a flood event, but data will be available that identifies small, frequent floods.

WATER FLOWS PERPENDICULAR TO THE SLOPE

Civil and hydrology engineers have developed very sophisticated methods for calculating runoff, times of concentration, peak flows, velocities, and other measures of flood events. They are able to map watersheds and subbasins. Major construction projects including dams, dikes, flood walls, and detention basins have been built to alleviate damage from storm water runoff, based on these procedures. The Army Corps of Engineers has been instrumental in developing the science of flood prediction and the craft of flood control. The Corps' prediction methods are applied within GIS, but they are outside the realm of planners and site designers. The advantage of GIS is that the engineering analysis can be merged with the planning analysis in a common environment.

GIS Drainage Maps

The best drainage operator available to designers is the application of a "cost surface algorithm" to an elevation map. This procedure begins at the high points on the site. Within each cell, the computer searches for the adjacent cell that has the greatest change in (lower) elevation. It will continue searching and moving until all drainage lines meet the edges of the study area. This process will not tell you whether the drainage is seasonal or whether there is a water source other than rainwater. It won't give you flood or erosion indicators. It serves only as an aid in design and can help in identifying surface variations, especially when they are not visible in the field, such as beneath heavy vegetation.

Viewsheds

The viewshed operator is a boon to design. A viewshed is the area that is visible from a given viewing point. The viewing point has three dimensions: $x, y,$ and z coordinates. The z coordinate is the height of the viewing point, not the ground elevation at that point. The computer sends a ray from the viewing point to the surrounding terrain. In essence, wherever the topography intersects the ray, the viewshed ends. In actuality, a vertical and horizontal cone is defined, so many rays are emitted. Because of this feature, viewsheds can be interrupted and resumed on a distant slope behind the interruption of the lower rays. Mature trees and forests may also be superimposed on the terrain, with heights that you describe, and these too can be used to define the viewshed. It is not at all uncommon to have summer and winter (leafless) viewsheds. As always, when possible, it is a good idea to field check the accuracy of some of the viewsheds.

What is the advantage of computer-generated viewsheds? They can be calculated from inaccessible viewing points, such as buildings not yet constructed nor even yet designed. Other inaccessible viewpoints may exist on properties not yet purchased, in extremely rugged terrain, over mining operations, over water, from highways not yet built, and so forth.

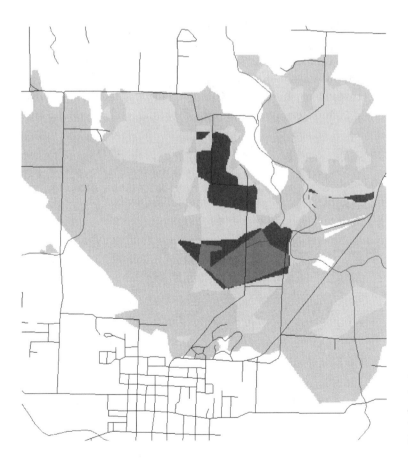

Figure 6.7 *A composite viewshed shows the visible areas from four viewing points. The darkest areas are visible from all four points.*

For example, if you are planning a visitor information center at a regional park, you can test the viewshed from ground level, atop a one-story building, or from a viewing platform. This assessment can be critical to the design of that facility. One may find a wonderful viewshed from the level of the second floor, but unattractive features may come into view at a higher level. The possibility of discovering unattractive views points to the need for a visual integrity study, which is discussed in the next section.

Possible screens can also be tested within viewshed studies to hide objectionable views, including views to proposed features such as parking areas and maintenance yards. This testing works the same as inserting an existing tree mass above. Other special codes have also been written that will indicate exactly the viewing height at which certain objects will become visible (Williamson and Liaw 1993).

A note worth mentioning has to do with study area size. You may not need all your coverages this large, but you should include topography, tree cover, roads, existing buildings, and parcel boundaries at least as far as the middle ground of your important viewsheds. The middle ground has been defined as one-quarter to three miles from the viewing point (Felleman 1986, 55). Often we define our study areas very narrowly and eliminate much of the viewshed, thus restricting the entire visual envelope with which we should be involved. The parcel boundaries theme is necessary if the project calls for land acquisitions or negotiation of conservation easements within important viewsheds.

Visual Integrity

INTEGRITY STUDIES REVEAL OUR VISUAL LEGACY

A visual integrity study combines a viewshed analysis with a map of visually objectionable features in the landscape. The operation begins by identifying the visually objectionable features, usually from a map of existing buildings and structures or from an aerial photo. Sometimes field work is required to make good assessments. Take into account the distance at which things will be viewed. They may look horrible at close range, but not so bad in the middle or background of the important viewsheds. It's the large elements, such as poultry production houses, major earthworks, or recycling (junk) yards that are especially hard to hide.

In working with historic units, like Civil War battlefields, not all existing structures may be objectionable. If the region was rural and agricultural at the time of the battle, there is nothing wrong with "old barns" in the view. The cattle may not be the same breed as in 1863, but only the purist will know the difference.

THE VISUAL INTEGRITY INDEX

Using the outline of a viewshed as a mask, the computer can count the number of objectionable features within its boundary. This mask and count constitute a "graphic overlay" operation. Different viewsheds, from different points or heights, can be compared for their visual integrity. Certain previously proposed viewpoints may be discarded based on this analysis.

The viewshed can be further divided into foreground, middle ground, and background, and a visual integrity map and report can be generated for each. Screens, such as vegetation, earth berms, or acceptable structures, can be inserted in the viewing area to define new viewsheds, and these new viewsheds can be compared for their integrity.

The viewshed operator is very valuable for land planning. There has also been a good deal of research about viewer preferences, especially in National Forests (Shannon et al. 1993; Hoffman and Palmer 1994; Clay 1996). There are some surprising results about preferences related to timber cutting and urban hillside development. Viewshed and visual integrity studies combined with documented preferences can build strong arguments for projects that may otherwise meet resistance. Even those not often swayed by logic have been known to cooperate when it is shown that a project can be implemented and they can protect their own viewshed as well.

Graphic Overlays—Combined Images

There are many times when we need to look at themes together, probably more often than not. For viewing or printing multiple themes, there are several options:

- The simple "overlay" operator will accomplish the visual overlay of any number of vector themes on one raster theme.
- To overlay two raster themes, select one to be on the bottom and it will show through the "no data" or "no value" portions of the top theme.
- Make one theme into a mask where the value areas or the nonvalue areas block out those portions of the image beneath it.
- Apply Boolean operators such as:
  A and not B, A and B, A or B, all but A and B, etc.
- Designate features to be overlaid from different themes by assigning preferences according to their database attributes.

Reclass and Recolor

When the data is entered, each theme has attributes that are noted in a table. Each attribute is given a reference number, and when a basic thematic map is queried, this is the number

Figure 6.8 Road and stream vectors are overlaid on a raster image showing historically significant areas.

shown on the screen. Then one goes to the "look-up table" to see the attribute that corresponds to that number. Some elements or features may generate several different themes and be listed in several attribute tables. For instance, streets may have a pavement theme, a bus route theme, and a traffic classification theme. Many databases are designed to let the designer see the attributes for all themes related to one element.

RECLASS CHANGES ASSIGNED CODE

Sometimes it is necessary to reassign the numbers attached to the attributes. Instead of using the default number assigned when the data was input, you might want to assign numbers as values, numbers that have meaning in a hierarchy or rating system. The "reclass" operator (called "recode" in some programs) allows one to change the number associated with the attributes, both in the look-up table and on the map.

Figure 6.9   A parcel map with eight attribute classes showing land value per acre.

It is often advantageous to group several attributes into a single new category or a few new categories. This grouping is easier to do in a raster format, but it can be accomplished with vectors. Usually this is done by first making a copy of the original map, as one would in CADD, then assigning the new classes (or codes) by their new reference numbers. The new map is then given a different name so as not to confuse it with the original map. (The computer will not allow two maps to have the same name.) A precaution: Give your maps really obvious names. If a dozen maps have been created with slightly different names, figuring out which one is needed can be very frustrating, especially if a few days have passed.

Reclass is essential when assigning suitability values, as when preparing a McHargian suitability overlay. Even though the final overlay operation for a McHarg suitability map is "map algebra," the individual themes are first assigned "suitability values" using the reclass operator.

Figure 6.10   The parcel map shown in Figure 6.9, reclassed into four attribute classes showing value per acre.

"Recolor" can be done for two basic reasons:

- To improve legibility in graphic overlays by making sure that when different themes are displayed simultaneously, each different element has a different color. Colors may also be changed within individual themes for greater clarity and visual appeal.
- To visually combine polygons on a map while maintaining more complexity in the attributes. (This will be discussed in Chapter 10 with a new graphic method of GIS site analysis.)

Buffers

Buffers can be used to create new maps and to generate quantities for design decisions. The typical buffer establishes a zone around a point, line, or polygon, based on a designated distance (and/or direction) from the element. The area within the buffer can be calculated, and features that fall within the buffer can be itemized or tallied.

SPHERES OF INFLUENCE

A very common buffer in our everyday lives is the right-of-way on either side of our roads. In some places the right-of-way extends 10 feet back from each face of curb, or 50 feet on either side of the centerline. For some types of analysis, like a quick calculation of right-of-way landscaping in order to develop maintenance estimates or to generate a mowing schedule, a buffer applied to streets is very handy.

Other GIS buffers may be established around all private residences or factories or alongside major roadways or railroads. These buffers may represent a privacy zone or a zone of increased noise, pollution, or hazard. Application of buffers is very common in wildlife habitat studies and in protection studies for sensitive plant communities. Buffers can also be defined by intersections with other themes such as watersheds or viewsheds. The beauty of the GIS is that if the assigned buffer takes away too much available land or is found to offer too little protection, it can be changed very quickly and new quantity takeoffs prepared. Decisions can be much easier to make and defend when we know fully the consequences of our proposals.

LandPlan Consultants of Tulsa, Oklahoma, use buffers to design trail systems. The firm proposes bike routes based on points of origin and destination and on calculations of the numbers of people to be served by alternate routes. Using census data, the designers determine the number of school-aged children who would use alternate routes from their homes to schools and parks, based on assigned buffer widths. "How many children live within four blocks of Proposal A versus Proposal B?" This GIS function adds important information that can be shared with citizens groups and planning boards in presenting design alternatives.

Map Algebra

Map algebra is actually many operators under one name. This group of operators is used to cause values assigned to various themes to be summed, or weighted and summed, as in the McHarg suitability analysis. Here is a summary of some simple

Figure 6.11   Buffer map from a single location showing all points within ¼ mile and all points within 1½ miles.

algebraic commands and algorithms that are common in spatial analysis:

- Add a common value to all values of a given theme.
- Divide all the values in a theme by a common divisor.
- Overlay themes and add values on a cell-by-cell or point-by-point basis (simple overlay).
- Multiply the values on one theme by a number, then add them to the values of another theme (weighted overlay).
- Select the reference number for each cell or location on a theme and use the instructions in a matrix to perform the assigned mathematical operation on each.
- Using the values shown in theme A, multiply them by the values of theme B in each location. For instance, if sensitive habitats exist on private lands and public lands, the public land value may be used as a multiplier to give a higher rating to sensitive habitats on public lands than on private lands (or vice versa).
- Use the values in a matrix to replace values of one or more themes. This replacement method is a quick way to reorganize priorities when a new objective has been given to the project or when other major changes have occurred.
- Overlay two themes and select the maximum value of the two.

Map algebra has many more options, and they vary from program to program. Algorithms are any map algebra functions used to simulate complex relationships and are applied in a uniform manner across one or more map surfaces. A cost surface is an example of an algorithm. Starting from a point, rays are sent in all directions. As a ray crosses a new cell (or point), it accumulates the assigned value of that cell (or point). Cost surfaces are used to determine routes for logging roads based on themes such as slope, rivers to cross, and erosive soils.

Models

If algorithms are bricks, models are walls. The complete set of instructions used to develop an analysis and/or synthesis is called a model. Two definitions of a GIS model are "a representation of reality" and "an attempt to duplicate nature in order to simulate, predict, or provide new information about physical and social features and processes" (Davis 1996, 311). The McHarg model is an example of a suitability model. It is one of the most widely used, and it includes the following steps:

1. Select relevant themes.
2. Assign values to attributes based on their suitability for the given activity (or use). This is a reclass, based on the experience and judgment of the designer.
3. Determine weighting for each theme.
4. Use map algebra to overlay themes, multiplying the values of the weighted themes, then adding the resultant values for each area or grid cell.
5. Recolor (or shade) the combined overlays to correspond to the resultant total values.
6. Identify those areas with lightest tones as most (or least) suitable for the proposed use. Quantify acreages of each suitability class.

Figure 6.12   Example of a suitability map based on the McHarg overlay method. Source: McHarg, Design with Nature *(New York: John Wiley & Sons, 1994).*

This model has been used around the world, for all types of studies, for three decades.

WHAT TYPE OF MODEL?

As with operators, models fall into classifications. Some of the names used to describe them are suitability models, environmental models, predictive models, sensitivity models, capability models, statistical models, and time series models. Of these, land planners most often use suitability, environmental, and predictive models.

SUITABILITY MODELS

Suitability models are most widely used by land planners and site designers. The goal is to evaluate the ability of lands to accommodate various uses. The suitability model may include evaluation of natural, political, economic, and cultural conditions. Landscape architects and land planners are trained to be generalists and to work with a variety of other design professionals. It is their ability to draw together disparate disciplines and points of view that makes them good facilitators. Using a variety of data themes, the suitability model calls into play judgments based on knowledge of local attitudes, established policies, economic realities, environmental science, and good development practices. The suitability model is quite flexible: it facilitates the convergence of points of view, and this interaction may account for its popularity.

Two examples of suitability studies are McHarg's *Plan for the Valleys of Baltimore County* (1969) and *Natural Habitats in the San Diego Region,* by the San Diego Association of Governments (SANDAG, 1995). The *Plan for the Valleys* was quite comprehensive and produced an Optimum Land Use proposal. The *Natural Habitats* study rated habitats according to vegetation types and identified habitats at risk owing to growth pressures in western San Diego County.

CAPABILITY MODELS

A similar type of model is the capability model. This model goes a step further in determining the carrying capacity of the land. With this model a measure of the impacts of the proposed uses is tested in order to meet a predetermined base line (such as

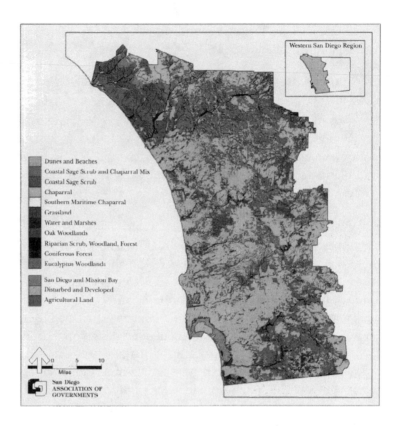

Figure 6.13 Vegetation theme for western San Diego County. This is one theme used in the county's habitats model. Source: INFO, *January-February 1995; SANDAG/SourcePoint, p. 14.*

sustaining minimum wildlife populations or not exceeding certain pollution levels). Such models tend to draw on scientific components, as in the environmental models.

AMERICAN AND DUTCH MODELS

In the United States the Natural Resources Conservation Service (NRCS) has developed a two-fold model to evaluate land capability. The Land Evaluation (LE) process identifies important agricultural lands, enabling planners to consider agricultural use in their decisions. NRCS also developed a Site Assessment (SA) process that examines the potential of a site for economic success based on its location relative to its market, taxes, and other factors. The LE rating is based primarily on soils, while the SA rating is based on planning issues. Together, the LESA rating is used in planning and farmland preservation (Steiner 1991, 135–139).

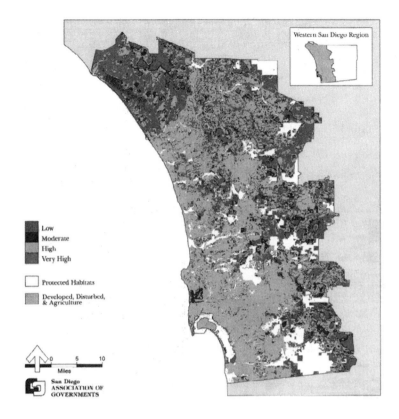

Low
Moderate
High
Very High

Protected Habitats

Developed, Disturbed,
& Agriculture

Western San Diego Region

0   5   10
Miles

San Diego
ASSOCIATION OF
GOVERNMENTS

*Figure 6.14   One resulting map
of the habitats suitability model.
Source: INFO, January-
February 1995; SANDAG/
SourcePoint, p. 15.*

   Planners in the Netherlands employ the McHarg suitability
method along with a capability classification system similar to
LESA. Further review places the subject site in the context of
possible future improvements, such as associated land reclamation (Steiner 1991, 145).

IN THE NATURAL REALM

Environmental modeling can involve subroutines from many
disciplines, including those of biologists, climatologists, soil scientists, chemical engineers (pollution models), dendrochronol-
ogists, hydrologists—and the list goes on. Environmental
models seek to recreate the processes that have brought the
study area to its current condition and those processes that are
ongoing. One goal of environmental modeling is to determine
possible impacts due to a proposed construction project or a
change in management practices.

Landscape architects and land planners are usually in the role of interpreting or detailing the proposed project. Often environmental modeling will lead to recommendations for mitigation, and again, site designers may play a role in refining those proposals.

PREDICTIVE MODELS

Predictive models "are used to test various scenarios ('what-if' cases) of proposed spatially related projects or processes" (Davis 1996, 317). A classic example is a comparison of alternate dam sites. Each model can be used to predict the extent of the reservoir impounded by the dam, the depth and total volume of the lake, and changes in land use and land cover. These comparisons can then be used for decision making.

REFERENCES

Antenucci, John C., Kay Brown, Peter L. Croswell, and Michael J. Kevany. 1991. *Geographic Information Systems: A Guide to the Technology.* New York: Van Nostrand Reinhold.

Burrough, Peter A. 1986. *Principles of Geographical Information Systems for Land Resources Assessment.* Oxford: Oxford University Press,

Clay, Gary. 1996. "Modeling Scenic Landscape Resources: An Integrated Approach at Articulating Color/Change Relationships in a High Elevation Forest in Southern Utah." *Earth Observation Magazine* (Aurora, CO), August.

Davis, Bruce E. 1996. *GIS: A Visual Approach.* Santa Fe, NM: Onword Press.

Felleman, John P. 1986. "Landscape Visibility." Chap. 4 in *Foundations for Visual Project Analysis,* edited by Richard C. Smardon, James F. Palmer, and John P. Felleman. New York: John Wiley & Sons.

Hoffman, Robin, and James F. Palmer. 1994. "Validity of Using Photographs to Simulate Visible Qualities of Forest Recreation Environments." *Council of Educators in Landscape Architecture Proceedings.* Starkville, MS: Mississippi State University.

Huxhold, William E. 1991. *An Introduction to Urban Geographic Information Systems.* New York: Oxford University Press.

Shannon, Scott, Jim Palmer, and Mary Anna Harrichak. 1993. "The Use of Digital Imaging in Assessing and Guiding U.S. Forest Service Visual Resource Management." In *CELA 93 Proceedings*. Eugene, OR: Council of Educators in Landscape Architecture.

Star, Jeffrey, and John Estes. 1990. *Geographic Information Systems: An Introduction*. Englewood Cliffs, NJ: Prentice-Hall.

Steiner, Frederick. 1991. *The Living Landscape*. New York: McGraw-Hill.

Tomlin, C. Dana. 1990. *Geographic Information Systems and Cartographic Modeling*. Englewood Cliffs, NJ: Prentice-Hall.

Williamson, Malcolm, and Chiou Guey Liaw. 1993. *Los.not*, computer routine written in GRASS; source code available at Center for Advanced Spatial Technologies, University of Arkansas, Fayetteville, AR.

WHERE DO I FIT IN THIS PICTURE?

It may appear that GIS is more suited to engineers and wildlife biologists than site designers. (That's like saying photography is meant for the rich and famous.) GIS can enrich your work just as it does theirs. It may open doors to new clients, new types of projects, or new ways of doing the work you're already known for. Chapter 7 hypothesizes the reasons that more site designers and land planners don't already use GIS. It's not a definitive review, but you may recognize some truth in it. Chapter 8 looks at some firms that are using GIS and how they are capitalizing on its benefits.

This book is not intended to make GIS'ers of us all. It is meant to explain the GIS domain and give you enough information that you may decide whether the technology is something you want to investigate further. It is intended to answer questions you may have had but didn't know how to ask or whom to ask. The goal is to help you make good decisions.

7

Why Aren't We Using GIS Now?

As a landscape architect, I have always been proud of this profession because it combines both science and art. While some among us decided against engineering for fear of the math, others shied away for fear of the tedium. Many of us seriously considered careers in art and decided that we wanted something more closely tied to the landscape (and we wanted real paychecks). Because this field spans the functions of both left brain and right brain, and because the name of our profession does not make our responsibilities especially clear, few people understand what we do or what value we add to a design team—that is, until they've worked with us. Studies have shown that our clients respect us, love our work, and think we make good team leaders. They also think we suffer from a lack of self-confidence (Bookout et al. 1994). What does this have to do with GIS?

As professional designers, we have obligations to society and to our clients. Our work is incredibly diverse. We must embrace new tools even if they do not fit our image of ourselves.

Many spatially oriented people, especially designers, and many land planners either are naturally right-brained or have trained themselves to become more so. Many people at decision-making levels in design firms did not grow up with computers. That lack of left-brain exposure leaves us with these issues:

- Computer phobia
- Unfamiliar-looking computer output
- Global, conceptual, nonlinear thinkers
- Differentiation between planning and design
- No Zen in computers

Some argue that these attributes have served us well in the past—"Why should we change now? Besides, we don't want young upstarts coming in and showing us up."

COMPUTER PHOBIA: STRUCTURE OR PRODUCT?

Those of us over the age of 40 had little or no exposure to computers before we entered college, and little access to them. When I was at the University of Michigan in the late 1960s, we used computers that filled a whole room in a special building. We each received a few hours of access time and very little instruction. There was nothing intuitive, graphic, or user friendly about those computers. One wrong keystroke could send our work to the abyss, and only engineering wizards could bring it back or even return us to square one where we could start over. With this introduction, it is no wonder that many of my generation became computer shy. It wasn't so much fear of failure as fear of total frustration. It felt like driving on a busy highway while blindfolded.

As computers improved their graphic user interfaces (GUIs), they became easier to use. As computer uses diversified from strictly business applications to word processing and simple record keeping, gradually more people saw a reason to get involved. When, in the early 1980s, computers began to show up in high school classrooms, it became obvious that computers were on their way to being an integral part of our society.

Youngsters Interface Early

Younger generations do have an advantage. Not only were their first computers much easier to use, they started using them at an earlier age, when work habits were not yet established. Computer use became second nature to them; it was integrated into their schoolwork as a tool, not a challenge.

My students are incredulous when I tell them that I completed college before hand-held calculators were invented. They stand aghast as I do long multiplication with a pencil. The calculators we used weighed more than 20 pounds and filled one end of a desk. No one bothers to check trig function reference books out of the library, and certainly no one buys them anymore; my students get trig functions out of their pocket calculators. Electronic technology envelops us.

The Standard Is Computerization

Most university design students today expect to have access to computers, scanners, printers, plotters, and digitizers. A large percentage own their own computers. At the University of Arkansas, all students in the School of Architecture are required to purchase a relatively high-powered computer in their second year. The school provides input and output devices, but the students purchase the basic computer, a monitor, and several software packages. Purchase of a computer is almost as commonplace as buying textbooks.

Baby-Boomers Catch Up

The more mature among us should not feel guilty or inferior about the gap in our computer skills. We can catch up; it is not impossible. The hardware and software are much easier to learn and use these days, and we have an advantage in knowing how to apply the technology. The computer tools are useless if one doesn't know what the goal is.

Changes for the Better

The other half of the computer phobia issue is the nature of the output. I recall the first time I saw a CADD drawing. It had no character. It was flat, lifeless, and cold. Everyone in the office agreed that it might be all right for engineers, but it would never do for landscape architects. Our work required vitality and depth. We relied on shadows and texture to give a three-dimensional quality to our drawings and renderings. Most of us had spent years improving our marker and colored pencil techniques. Our color choices were part of our signature.

Two things have changed: the computer's ability to vary its output, and our perception of computer-generated drawings. First, there are a number of software packages designed to enhance the output of other software. CADD or GIS drawings can be imported into enhancement packages such as Fractal Painter or even the commonly available PowerPoint. These packages have many more colors, textures, and techniques to enhance the images. Some packages have new techniques that apply fill patterns unevenly, as with an airbrush. Tree shadows need not be cookie-cutter replicas. Vegetation can acquire irregular patterns representing fine- or coarse-textured leaves. Even lettering can be made to look as if it were done by hand. Several fonts have been developed that have a "manual style."

Second, we have adjusted to the computer-generated look. It has permeated graphic design, packaging, and product design. It's been around so long there is now a counter-computer style, even though its images are also produced on a computer. Industry has fully recognized the advantages of speed, modification, and consistent output that the computer offers. Virtually every image, text, pattern, and color we see today was manipulated or generated by a computer. Chapter 8 reviews a survey that included questions about the public's perception of computer-generated graphics. It suggested that today everyone is used to the look of computer output.

GLOBAL, CONCEPTUAL, NONLINEAR THINKERS

Designers and planners are trained to have multiple points of view. Our knowledge is broad and only moderately deep. We each have areas of specialization in which we have conducted research, experimented with theories, and developed our own set of responses to particular problems; but we remain generalists rather than specialists. This broad base of knowledge has tended to separate us from the computer, where software packages have very specific operators and many of them require strict mathematical approaches and detailed knowledge of certain functions, such as statistical distribution and hydrologic modeling. The scientists earned an early advantage in putting the computer to work for them, and thus it was designed for them.

Further, the slow development of graphic user interfaces deterred design professionals, as well as the general public, for a full decade before Apple released its first Macintosh computers. Not until the release of Windows 95 did the DOS world have a really effective GUI. The software manuals have been notoriously undecipherable, spawning a whole industry of do-it-yourself training manuals. Tutorials have improved somewhat, but for years they were too streamlined and were offered out of context for real projects.

Finally, the computer world is changing, to our advantage. Not only are the programs much more user friendly, the operating systems also have improved GUIs. Windows 95 did not accidentally emulate the Macintosh operating environment; anyone can see the advantages of point-and-click. If you've held out this long, now is a good time to finally become computerized.

Digital Transfer: A Revolving Door

Another huge advantage for conceptual thinkers is digital transfer. There are now many protocols for moving text, graphics, and images from one software package to another. Desktop publishing packages allow you to pull text from one program, diagrams and charts from another, and photos from still another. Even within programs, the individual operators are becoming much more diverse. Microsoft Word has a small but flexible set of graphics tools embedded in it. Ten years ago word processing programs did one thing: word processing. The interoperability of almost all programs has improved, and GIS is no exception.

Do It Your Way!

The technique that is the focus of this book also takes advantage of digital transfer. Although you can do all of the "design operations" within a GIS package, it is much easier to add the bubble diagrams and labels in a graphics program. Once the analysis and notes have been added, the files are transferred back into the GIS, where the three-dimensional drape is produced (see Chapter 10). Just the fact that the files can be transferred easily makes life so much better for all of us. It allows us to use the approach we have used all of our professional lives. We are not required to reduce our work to mathematic equations in order to work in a computer environment.

Use Your Software, Not Just Theirs

Digital file transfer has further implications for design offices. It also means that an office can use a program that is different from those of others on a design team, and usually the files will be compatible with one another. If the civil engineer is using AutoCADD, the landscape architect can reasonably expect to import Microstation files back and forth between the offices. This transfer is not always flawless, but it is possible and improving all the time.

Interoperability Standards

Officially since May 1993, and unofficially before that, the Open Geographic Information Systems consortium (OGIS) has been studying ways to make all files transferable between programs. OGIS has strong linkages to the GIS standards community, which works with software developers to incorporate "open architecture" to facilitate greater transferability. This development is very good news for generalists.

PLANNING IS NOT DESIGNING

Another debate within the fields of land planning, urban planning, landscape architecture, engineering, biological sciences, earth sciences, and architecture is the role of the computer in site design. Site design differs from land planning in its scale and level of detail. Site design assigns specific uses, with their attendant facilities, to locations on one or more parcels of land. Planning assigns broad uses, without facilities recommendations, to study areas made up of many properties. Planning is tied to zoning, land use ordinances, and other policies, but facilities are secondary in planning proposals. Physical expression is integral to site design.

Landscape architects, engineers, and architects think of CADD as the "end all, be all" for site design. Three-dimensional programs, like Form Z, LandCADD, or CADD modules, such as Intergraph Corporation's Terrain Analyst, or other terrain analysis programs, are used to visualize sites and study areas from bird's-eye perspectives. These are appropriate tools for site design and visualization. But they're not the only tools.

Originally, the planners and scientists were the ones using GIS. For many years, the design community felt that the effort required to collect the data, the cost of GIS equipment and software, the lengthy training associated with GIS, and the complexity of GIS operators were justified only for large, regional, or urban studies. Once these excuses were valid, but no longer.

GIS Crosses Over to Design

Not only is GIS software becoming more user friendly, GIS hardware is also becoming more friendly. One no longer needs a UNIX workstation to operate a robust GIS. At the same time, hardware is becoming more powerful for less money. Today's hardware also has more storage capacity and friendlier operating systems. The cost of hardware has dropped dramatically in recent years, and the amount of competition provides an optimistic outlook for future prices. Couple racier equipment with widely available data, and the phrase "appropriate technology" applies to a much broader range of project types. Where regional planning was once the only appropriate project type for GIS, subdivision and park master planning are now done in a GIS with regularity.

It is now reasonable to consider a GIS for site design. It may not be appropriate for all sites, but it should be considered. Add to this equation a GIS process that emulates that of traditional site designers, and it becomes a very viable alternative. Chapter 10 lays out such a process in step-by-step detail. The advantages of quantification and report generation, of direct 3-D modeling, and of combining diverse types of data and analyses make GIS the most advanced tool available to today's site designers.

ZEN IN DESIGN

The loss of Zen in design may be the real crux of the matter. When we design, our creative juices are flowing. We are thoroughly involved in the act of designing, we concentrate deeply on what we are doing, and we can interact only with others who are focused on the same issues. There is a gestalt that makes design exciting. It is difficult to maintain this connection with our subconscious creativity while speaking a foreign language. To many, the computer is a foreign language, one not very familiar to them.

What is proposed in Chapter 10 does not make the design process itself computerized. The act of placing program bubbles and arrows on a site analysis is done manually. It is done within the setting of a computer, but the design act is not directed by the computer: it is done with the manual strokes of a mouse or a computer pen. It can first be done on tracing paper with a pencil or marker and then drawn in the computer. There is no translation from abstract spatial ideas to Boolean logic; what you see is what you get.

The site analysis described in Chapter 10 follows GIS procedures. The step-by-step process is easy to follow, and the resulting site analysis looks like one you would create at your drawing board. This site analysis is a stand-alone, readable image. You do not need to recall what conditions were assigned what values: the image is legible as it is. This legibility allows you to draw your bubble diagrams directly on the site analysis. No translation is required.

The ARS "tint over photo" and the optional terrain drape are the prepared for presentation purposes. Next, the ARS is moved into a CADD environment for the preliminary design. The design steps are still largely manual. In 1995 five teams participated in a design charette using computers, at the ASLA Annual Convention held in Cleveland, Ohio. In a *Landscape Architecture* magazine article, J. William Thompson said, "But if inventory and analysis demonstrated the superiority of computer applications in certain areas, design development demonstrated precisely the opposite. During the search for design alternatives, every single team turned its back on the computer and reverted to pencil and tracing paper." This return to hand-and-eye methods should demonstrate that one need not use the computer when it is not appropriate. You can decide when to use it and when not to. The Zen is still there!

REFERENCES

Bookout, Lloyd W., Michael P. Beyard, and Steven W. Fader. 1994. *Value by Design.* Washington, DC: Urban Land Institute.

Thompson, J. William. 1996. "Reconsidering the Cutting Edge." *Landscape Architecture,* January.

8

Who Is Using GIS in the Design Professions?

GIS in land planning is being used by 150-person firms and 3-person offices. Engineers and landscape architects use GIS in site design for subdivision layouts, resort designs, and park master plans. Landscape architects use GIS to conduct visual analyses for ski resorts and mining reclamation proposals and for trail and greenway designs. GIS is used for master planning of Civil War battlefields. Each year new applications are found for GIS. In this chapter we review a small, informal survey conducted by the author to explore this question. Responses came from landscape architects, planners, engineers, and government agencies, from coast to coast.

SURVEY QUESTIONS AND RESPONSES

Question 1. Describe the primary uses of GIS in your firm (or agency). What types of projects use GIS? What questions are answered by GIS?

Most of the landscape architecture firms with active GIS programs use them for regional planning, resort planning, park master planning, trails planning, natural resource management, viewshed analysis, and mapping (without analysis). It seems that natural systems are addressed with GIS more often than social systems, at least among landscape architecture firms, eight of which were included in the poll. Engineering firms are using it for site planning related to large developments; four such firms were included in this survey. Engineers and planners also work with public works departments and tax assessors to estimate costs and revenues with GIS. Public agencies primarily distribute data to local governments and private consultants; six such agencies were interviewed.

Here are some of their responses. First are responses from landscape architecture firms:

"We use GIS for transportation planning analysis, studying potential numbers of users for new bus routes and drive times, habitat management and preservation, looking at critical habitat, risk levels and bio-diversity. Mapping for large scale-planning: CADD conversion to geo-mapping, for decisions about adjacent uses."

"Regional planning, mountain planning, PUDs, some site scale design."

"We use it for trail planning; matching up origins with destinations such as schools, parks, and medical facilities."

"We have several types of GIS projects: watershed management, land use, resource management. Other regional planning such as consolidation of scattered parcels for the BLM. International work includes study of environmental constraints and suitability mapping, mostly for development, resorts, and coastal development. For environmental assessment and EIS preparation, mostly for water resource and land use issues. We also do viewshed mapping and facility siting with GIS."

"Land planning: mostly in rural areas for developers or even individual owners. Parks and recreation planning, for the National Park Service."

"Large-scale regional planning projects—especially those with natural elements."

Responses from engineering firms:

"We do mapping with GIS and site suitability analysis. We look at future land uses and fiscal impacts; yield of taxes and costs with different scenarios."

"We're doing airport noise studies with GIS, and management planning for the airport. We're planning to work with the city on street layouts. We're also planning on getting in on some recreation planning with GIS."

"We use it for locating utilities and roadways, for wetlands mitigation, for tax parcels and address matching. Our planning division uses GIS for some quick-and-dirty land use/land cover stuff, but that's it. Our landscape architecture division doesn't use GIS at all. The environmental engineers here use it for assessment of hazardous waste sites."

Responses from government agencies about the kind of work they do:

"We work with the 23 towns in our service area here in central Vermont. We provide maps such as utilities, transportation, natural resources. We do some suitability mapping, but mostly it's inventory; land use/land cover, base mapping for tax maps."

"We have data ad nauseum. We act as a liaison to federal information systems. We serve Boston and 51 affiliate offices with data."

"Our work is quite variable. The urban counties use it for zoning, land use, emergency dispatch, transportation systems. They go after grants from the State of Wisconsin."

"We serve the 11 state departments and the county boards."

"We do GIS ourselves. Typical projects include calculating acres of each land use, how many trips are generated by that land use; we forecast housing needs and employment; we generate land use statistics."

"We use GIS for growth forecast, demographic mapping, employment mapping, damage assessment, property identification, eco-regions mapping. It's used to develop general plans and determine political districts."

Question 2. What types of clients use GIS? Are they public agencies, and if so, what level of government do they represent? Are there private clients?

Overwhelmingly, most GIS work is done for public clients, but at many levels of government. The landscape architecture firms have more of a balance of public and private clients because they do GIS work for residential, mixed-use, and resort developers. Those public agencies that do GIS analysis themselves use in-house expertise or contract with a variety of outside consultants.

Surprisingly, several landscape architects said that their public clients did not require them to use GIS. They said they used it because it was more efficient, especially when working with other disciplines. (The survey did not ask the question, "Do you actively pursue GIS projects?")

Landscape architects' responses regarding their GIS clients:

"Most of our clients are public, some developers use GIS."

"Developers."

"All public clients—cities."

"State agencies."

"Public utilities, military, BLM, Bureau of Reclamation, Forest Service, municipal governments. Firmwide, maybe 50% are private developers."

"Counties, international agencies, private planning and engineering firms, the Nature Conservancy."

"Both public and private."

"About 60% public, 40% private."

Responses from engineering firms, describing their clients:

"More public than private."

"Municipalities."

"I work for mayors, small cities mostly. And for developers, for residential and mixed-use developments."

Responses from agencies, naming their customers:

"We serve the cities in our consortium."

"We get requests from cities and counties."

"Counties and private users."

"Seventy-two counties in the state of Wisconsin."

"Washington County, Vermont, plus three towns."

"Mostly state agencies, and municipal affiliates."

Question 3. Describe the model you use. Is it a McHargian overlay, weighted overlays, or network analysis? Have you developed other models or do you work with other disciplines that use other models?

The McHarg overlay method seems to be widely used for land planning. See Chapters 6 and 10 for a review of the McHarg model. There is some interaction with other disciplines, which has broadened the spectrum of model types used indirectly in land planning.

Several firms use no models at all. They use the GIS only to assemble and produce inventory maps, without analysis.

Landscape architects' responses about their models:

"Some are more sophisticated than McHarg. We use weighted overlays, reclasses at break points."

"Weighted overlays."

"We develop our own suitability models. We often include public perception as part of the equation. We use viewshed analysis, terrain analysis. We also work with other professionals and link to their models: hydrography, fire modeling, fish hatcheries."

"McHarg overlays for our work. We also work with civil and structural engineers, biological scientists, ecologists, economists, environmental consultants."

"We always use McHarg for public clients: to do opportunities and constraints mapping. We have also used predictive models to test a range of alternative futures. Physical suitability mapping for things like slopes for trails or other thresholds."

"McHargian models. We might throw a twist on it by changing the rankings."

"Weightings with market analyst, queries on information to create new layers, turning layers on and off."

Engineers' descriptions of their models:

"For land use it's weighted overlay. But we also use environmental modeling, storm water management and sediment loading models."

"We don't use any models. We don't do analysis or suitability mapping. We just do mapping."

"Overlays."

Most of the government agencies only provide data. Those who do in-house analysis primarily use McHarg overlays.

Question 4. Has your work been presented to citizens groups? As compared with hand-drawn maps, how are the computer-generated maps received by the public? How is the accuracy of the maps perceived by the public?

Most respondents were of the opinion that the public prefers computer-generated maps to hand-drawn maps. We did not discuss subtleties such as display size relative to room size, room lighting, or paper types. Two landscape architects thought that hand-drawn maps were preferred, and they enhance their computer output with colored pencils.

Most respondents stated unequivocally that the public was more willing to accept the accuracy of the computer maps. However, this question of perceived accuracy brought several unsolicited remarks, such as, "It really doesn't make sense. They should realize that there can be mistakes in this data, just as there are in hand-drawn maps." Yet almost everyone agreed that computer-generated maps received far less scrutiny than hand-drawn maps.

Landscape architects' responses:

"Yes, the public is usually pleased with computer-generated maps. They don't question the work; we present the imagery and the method and the citizens accept it."

"They love the GIS maps, especially the colors."

"Yes, at a public forum. The GIS maps had been enhanced to look like hand-drawn maps and the response was the same."

"Yes, good reception, beautiful and clear maps. Regarding perceived accuracy there are very few problems, no credibility problems, there's total acceptance. It was done by a computer—it must be right."

"We've done a lot of public presentations. The public likes computer-generated maps. They think they are more accurate."

"They receive it much, much better. We have been very innovative in public participation. We use several survey methods, such as 'community will' and other consensus technologies."

"Usually they're more impressed. The maps are easier to read; it's easy to change scale, colors, patterns. The perceived accuracy is probably about the same as with hand-drawn maps."

"They prefer the hand-drawn maps, especially for PUDs or subdivisions—both plan views and perspectives. People perceive it [GIS] to be more accurate than it is. They think it's gospel truth. The data's not too bad, but they think it's perfect."

Engineers' responses regarding perception of map appearance and accuracy:

"The clarity of the drawing is better with GIS; the public understands it well. Clients can be dazzled. It's sometimes hard to get people to focus on the issues."

"Citizens respond favorably. The output looks nicer, more formal."

"The airport board has presented the maps. The folks were more interested in noise levels than maps. They didn't agree with the noise level shown at their houses. They didn't feel the color assignment was accurate."

"Citizens like computer maps better. They accept them better."

Question 5. Describe the backgrounds of the personnel in your office who use GIS. Are they landscape architects or planners who have learned to use GIS themselves (either in school or after); or are they experienced landscape architects or planners

Among landscape architecture and planning firms, the preference seems to be design professionals who also have GIS skills. Every firm interviewed had some people meeting that description. There are also a number of decision makers, experienced landscape architects, or planners, who work with the GIS experts in their offices.

When agencies do planning or design work in-house, it is done by experienced planners, either in concert with a GIS technician or by using their own GIS skills. Data transfer is done by GIS technicians, some of whom are cartographers or geographers.

Landscape architects' responses:

"In this firm I do most of the GIS work. I have a landscape architecture degree from Cal Poly, and that's where I learned GIS as well. There are two other people who are not LAs, and they do data input and remedial work. There are probably eight or ten landscape architects who are project managers, and they work with me on GIS projects."

"One and the same. I'm a landscape architect, and I taught myself to do GIS."

"The project manager is an experienced landscape architect. The most experienced GIS person here graduated from the University of Arkansas. She got some GIS training there and has taught herself MapInfo and ArcView here in the office."

"Firmwide, all offices, there are probably 12 GIS technicians, 15 other computer technicians, 10 people who are planners or LAs and know GIS themselves, and perhaps 100 LAs and environmental planners who use GIS but cannot sit at the computer and give GIS commands."

"Three landscape architects who have also taught themselves ArcView."

"The byte cave is gone. Now the landscape architects and planners do their GIS work themselves."

"Two LAs with GIS skills, eight LAs and planners without."

Engineering firms' responses about their GIS personnel:

"Out of about fifty on staff, four or five are GIS technicians. All the others work with them."

"Staff are environmental scientists, all with GIS abilities. Ten altogether."

"We just hired a GIS technician. Previously we had an engineer who did GIS for us."

"We're a 110-person firm and 4 of us use GIS. Two are GIS technicians, AutoCADD and surveyor types. The others are an engineer and a hydrogeologist."

Few agency personnel who use GIS have design backgrounds:

"We have about 25 people; most have a background in geography or cartography. A few are earth scientists or planners. No landscape architects. We have a few engineering technicians."

"The planners are expected to learn GIS themselves."

"We have 70 permanent people and another 10 to 20 temporary people. Of these, 20 do research and 15 of them use ArcInfo. In the transportation division there are 20 people, of which 8 use ArcInfo."

"One GIS technician, with a cartography degree, one land use planner who does GIS, and one transportation planner who uses GIS. We usually have summer interns who write macros [commands]. They get formal plus on-the-job training."

Question 6. What do you feel are the major advantage and major disadvantage of GIS?

Several advantages were recognized. The most commonly mentioned advantage is the ability to combine complex and disparate types of information in problem solving. It was noted that this ability to merge input is especially helpful in working on multidisciplinary teams.

Depending on the software, the capability exists to import CADD files into the GIS environment. Thus, CADD data such as utilities, street centerlines, or building footprints can be imported and used with GIS raster or vector datasets such as soil types or census tract boundaries. It was suggested that this CADD data conversion is of real benefit in expanding the available data and that if the CADD drawings are generated in-house, the data can be trusted. Several people commented that they import AutoCADD files into ArcView on a regular basis.

The ease of iterations was mentioned several times. This agility gives designers the option to ask "what if?" and to test several alternative approaches. GIS allows such testing to be done quickly and inexpensively. Clients are greatly impressed with this testing capability. The measure and report functions included in GIS applications give quantities of any mapped condition, which in turn can be used to quickly generate cost estimates, yields, or carrying capacities.

Another noted advantage is the ability to change the look of the image. The ability to change scale in order to print maps of different sizes was mentioned repeatedly. Color tables can be easily adjusted, labels changed, lines modified. The experience of the authors and two of the respondents is that colors are easily changed in GIS, but other elements such as text and lines are changed much more easily and with more choices outside the GIS environment. It is usually not difficult to export an image from the GIS software into a graphics application (such as Adobe Photoshop or Microsoft Powerpoint) for finishing the maps.

Good Data Is Often Hard to Find

The disadvantage noted most often was the data dilemma. When accurate data at an appropriate resolution is available, all is well. When data is not available, or it has inconsistencies, GIS is very difficult to use as it can raise doubts among all the design professionals.

Another disadvantage is the cost, mostly for obtaining good data. Other costs include hardware, software, and training. The learning required for some types of software is much greater than for others.

Landscape architects' responses:

"Advantages: Can work through complex issues with much less effort. It allows you to be creative about communications.

The disadvantage is people expect automatic turnaround times."

"Once you have a good database, you can access the information very quickly, and the analysis is very quick. The hard part is getting accurate data."

"Advantages: It forces you integrate information from a variety of sources. It makes everyone [on the design team] talk to each other. It gives clarity, good analytical support for decisions. Disadvantages: It is perceived by some to be complex, difficult, and expensive."

"Speed and accuracy are great. No disadvantages."

"The major advantage is that you can redefine opportunity costs through testing. You can harness the iterative capability of GIS. Disadvantage: There's no Zen about it; it separates the operator from the data."

"It's so malleable; it gives you the ability to portray many types of info in many ways. The disadvantage: Sometimes you need more site-specific information; it's hard to get good site data; you have to dig deeper, do more field checking— but that's the same for any project."

"Advantage: Integrative capacity; drawing from many sources at different scales and being able to combine them. Disadvantage: Clients want maps redone over and over."

"The amount of information and flexibility are great, the speed with which you can retrieve data. The disadvantage is in creating an accurate database. You need field verification."

Engineers' responses were very similar:

"Advantages: Time savings, multiple iterations, quick and easy amendments, reduction and enlargement capabilities for reports and presentations. Disadvantages: It's become inexpensive, so too many businesses are getting into GIS. Many inappropriate operators are producing GIS products, and they're telling the wrong story."

"You can get in and do things a lot faster. Being able to combine so many sources of data is a plus, and the fact that they are geo-referenced and have intelligence. The disadvantage is that not enough people understand it, and some of the people who are doing it don't know what they're doing."

"Advantages: If the data is there, the speed of analysis is terrific. The disadvantage is cost."

"You can quickly get answers and pose different questions. The different scales and multiple maps are advantages. It takes time to learn the software."

Only two agencies responded to this question:

"Advantages: The ability to manipulate data, update maps and produce maps at variable scales. It works for towns or regions. Disadvantages: Large cost to develop data. This is an intangible; it's difficult to quantify up front."

"Allows more 'what-if' analyses."

Question 7. In your opinion, how is GIS affecting land planning?

This question brought out exuberance in many participants. Most people believe strongly that GIS is affecting planning in a positive way. They think that better decisions are being made because they are based on more information. They think that GIS has allowed different disciplines to communicate better with one another. The public agency people sense that communities are taking a much more active role in their own planning decisions. There seems to be widespread optimism about the future of GIS.

Landscape architects responses:

"GIS is benefitting land planning, but it sometimes gets misused. Some people will twist things around to the way they view them. Some people have ethics. It can separate people from the work, if they don't have the new skills they need. Most landscape architecture grads with GIS skills go to work for engineering or environmental firms."

"It isn't affecting it. It's good with a flat site. You can't do Calthorpian designs with it."

"It is affecting the results positively—people are making better decisions. It has value for parks master planning. You can play 'what if'."

"It's still very early. The data isn't there yet, or it's too expensive. It can greatly impact land planning, as agencies are better set."

"It's supporting credibility, speeding things up, making things more systematic. GIS is here to stay; it's in the mainstream."

"It's a more people-friendly tool. All the agencies will accept GIS."

"GIS holds the promise to get at comprehensiveness. You can use it to ascertain impacts, devise a common value system, model ecology. You can put a price tag on clean air and water."

"GIS enhances the field; so much more is available to people. Things are becoming more streamlined."

Responses of two engineers:

"Positively, it's a tremendous asset. Communities are coming on board. Those with tax parcel information are really excited."

"In this area not at all—there's not much demand for GIS here."

Agency staff were probably most excited about the changes they have seen as a result of the introduction of GIS:

"Parcel mapping at the local level has mushroomed. Communities are really getting involved in their own future."

"Not nearly well enough yet. Land use planning is a growth area. There's a need for more analytical work. Here in Wisconsin data is available. Visualization will be important."

"It's making planners look at things in more detail. It allows us to look at sophisticated data quickly."

"It has increased public awareness of data. The Department of Transportation just throws money at planning now."

"Positively: Towns are more aware of relationships of different aspects of their town. People are more aware of possibilities of what they can do with maps. They expect quality and accuracy. Most towns rely on maps for making decisions. The general public might not know about planning, but the local governments do."

SUMMARY OF FINDINGS

The conclusion of this brief survey is that GIS is becoming an integral part of land planning.

- Where data is readily available, GIS work is plentiful (see Chapter 5).
- GIS software is getting easier to learn and to use.
- It's better to have a design professional using GIS directly instead of working with a GIS technician, but using a GIS technician also works.
- The computer equipment is getting less expensive and easier to maintain.
- The public likes the look of computer maps and trusts the accuracy of the data.
- Agencies that have data must use it to justify the funding for it. Many cities are deeply committed to GIS.
- GIS work includes large-scale planning as well as site design for resorts, parks, and subdivisions.

HOW CAN I USE GIS WITHOUT A BASIC CHANGE IN MY DESIGN APPROACH?

The consideration to begin using geographic information systems is a serious one. To use GIS successfully, you must build on your strengths, not your weaknesses. That is the reason that the process described in Chapter 10 was developed. It was designed to give landscape architects and other site designers the ability to use the GIS tool without abandoning the process they have used for years. It adapts GIS technology to the methods we were taught and that we continue to use for a great diversity of projects. The leopard doesn't need new spots; he needs sunglasses.

Chapter 9 reviews the site design process on which Chapter 10 is based. Your site design process may vary from this one, but at least you will know how it varies, and we hope that this knowledge will help you avoid confusion.

Design Process—The Old-Fashioned Way

The main purpose of this book is to share a new approach to using GIS. It is based on the idea that work can be done in a GIS environment that follows the same design procedures you already use and with results that you can understand.

Let us review the basic design process most of us use, so you can follow as it is incorporated in the GIS techniques that follow. Your own procedure may vary, but the one discussed here is the basis for the GIS process described in Chapter 10. You may decide to modify it slightly to match your own approach more closely.

Keep Your Eye on the Ball

The design process begins with goals and objectives. Usually the client has established the goals and has most of the objectives fixed in his or her mind. It is our job to evaluate and suggest revisions or expansions. Of course, the final decision is the client's. A clear set of goals and objectives will lead to a sound program of uses.

And on the Bottom Line!

The client's program may come to us fully developed, or less so. If the client is a seasoned developer or a time-tested agency chief, that person will draw from his or her own experience to develop a program of uses to be implemented. Many developers, especially commercial and residential developers, rely heavily on market analysts to determine the size of the residential lots or how much rent to charge retail tenants. All of this quantification will manifest itself in amenities and project budgets. If the client does not have outside help in refining the program, then the designer may take on that role, recognizing the limitations of his or her abilities. Most of us are not trained to calculate demand or generate feasibility studies with revenue expectations or amortization schedules.

THE PROGRAM

Begin With Uses, Not Facilities

We rely on experience or research, or both, when refining a program. There are many excellent publications about specialty areas of design: resorts, golf courses, office campuses, botanical gardens, and custom residences. Many practices specialize in

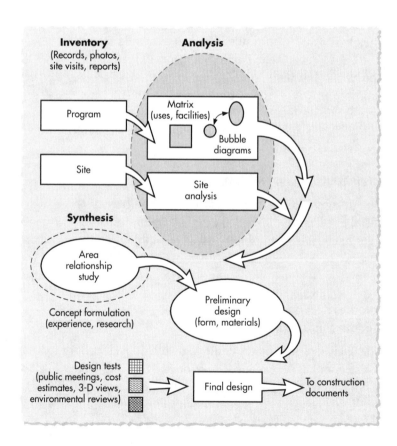

Figure 9.1 Site design process: This diagram shows sequence of steps in the design process. Any step or group of steps can be repeated as needed when new information is introduced or when the deisgner wants to test new ideas.

one or more of these areas, and their clients come to them as much for definition of goals, objectives, and programs as for their design skills. The types of information used to refine a program include:

- Descriptions of primary and support facilities needed to accommodate each activity
- Definition of minimum space for each activity and facility
- Description of the desirable spatial qualities associated with the activity or related facilities, and conditions to be avoided
- Current local demand for the activities or opposition to them
- Identification of user groups
- General costs of implementation, operation, and maintenance
- Possible environmental or cultural impacts of the activity

The program analysis can take several forms, among which are:

- Decision matrices (and/or descriptive matrices)
- Bubble diagrams

The purpose of a matrix is to summarize the results of the research or the basis for decisions made during program definition. The proposed use (and/or facility) will always make up one axis. The other axis may be one or more of the items listed earlier: desirable conditions, user groups, costs, and the like. In this case the matrix becomes the list of ground rules to be used later in the design process. This list of rules tells the client, and/or the public, the assumptions under which you were working when preparing the site analysis and area relationship study.

In their benchmark work on problem solving, Don Koberg and Jim Bagnall state, "Matrix interrelationships may be shuffled until groups or large patterns become clear. The large pattern relationships might then be studied as essential overall definition possibilities" (1972, 62).

The matrix can also be used as a selection or elimination table. Say, for instance, that a total of 17 uses are proposed by several sources, but they won't all fit on the site, or the client can't afford all of them. The matrix can be used to record scores or rankings for one or several criteria. The different sources may assign different scores to each criteria. Thus, you may have an evaluation of each use from the point of view of the owner, the reviewing agency, the neighbors, and the lending institution. (You may record these scores in the matrix based on comments made at meetings or in interviews, correspondence, or reports.) The total scores or rankings can then be used to eliminate the less desirable activities. It is important to share these matrices with your client before showing them to anyone else.

Proposed Recreation Use	Evaluation Criteria	A. Appropriate to site	B. Supply and demand ratio	C. Desirability to community	D. Relative cost to implement	E. Relative cost to maintain	F. Revenue generation potential	TOTAL	SELECTED USES
TRAILS									
1. Hiking trails		3	2	3	3	2	0	13	•
2. Equestrian trails		3	3	3	3	1	0	13	•
OVERNIGHT USES									
3. Primitive camping		2	1	1	2	1	0	7	
4. RV camping		2	3	0	0	0	3	8	
5. Equestrian camping		2	3	0	0	0	3	8	
DAY USES									
6. Family picnicking		3	3	2	2	2	0	12	•
7. Group picnicking		3	3	1	2	2	0	11	•
8. Outdoor lecture theater		3	1	1	3	3	0	11	•
9. Ball fields		1	2	1	2	1	0	7	

Figure 9.2 Decision matrix: One type of program analysis matrix is set up to evaluate the proposed uses against several criteria.

Bubbles, Bubbles Everywhere

The term *bubble diagram* has been used to describe two different points in the design process, and that duplication has caused some confusion. In this book, bubble diagram refers to the idealized arrangement of uses that are generated without regard to any particular site. The term *area relationship study,* or ARS, is used to describe the drawing that fits the uses (shown as bubbles) on the site analysis. At the ARS stage the spatial arrangement of the bubbles has to be adjusted to fit the site, and they may no longer be "idealized"; they may not retain the perfect symmetry (or the perfect nesting, etc.) they had at the earlier stage. Some people refer to this later ARS image as "the bubble diagram," and thus the confusion begins. The ARS is a bubble diagram, but it has been adjusted to existing site conditions. In this book, bubble diagram refers to the initial arrangement of program uses, in an idealized sense; the ARS refers to the adaptation of the idealized bubble diagram to the site analysis.

The purpose of the programmatic bubble diagram is to examine the ideal spatial relationships between the various uses and their associated program linkages. For instance:

- Should one use be close to another or separated by a distance or by a physical barrier?
- Proportionally, what are the size relationships of the various uses to one another? The bubble diagram is abstract, so there is no scale or absolute size. Is one use about twice as large as another, or half as large?
- How many types of circulation routes are there? Here are some choices: pedestrian, user vehicular, service vehicular, emergency vehicular, user physically challenged, day user, overnight user. Each circulation type should be shown on the bubble diagram with a different line symbol. Heavily used circulation routes will be shown with heavy lines and lighter traffic patterns with thinner lines. Vehicular use may be shown with solid lines, pedestrian use with dashed or dotted lines. Arrows on both ends of a line may indicate two-way traffic.
- Certain uses may have views associated with them (such as outdoor dining or a scenic overlook). The need for

good views should also be indicated on the idealized bubble diagram.

There can and should be several workable bubble diagrams. Some bubble diagrams will be flawed, but several or many will be acceptable. One or two may be "perfect." Don't quit generating bubble diagrams too soon.

Site Organizational Concepts

Spatial concepts can also be represented in bubble diagrams, although this application of an ordering method is not always necessary. Some perfectly functional bubble diagrams will have no identifiable organizational concept. Some concepts of site organization show the uses as being arranged in any of the following ways:

- Linear fashion
- Central uses with peripheral circulation
- Central primary uses with secondary uses at a distance on all sides, either arranged as satellites around the moon or in a radial pattern

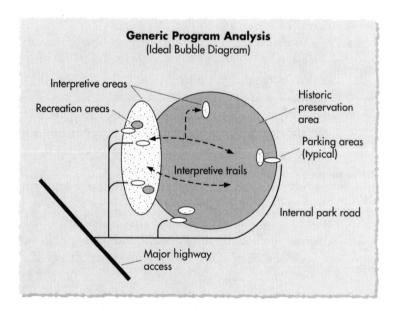

Figure 9.3 *The Idealized bubble diagram shows each use and its spatial relationships and linkages to all other uses. Several different bubble diagrams should be explored. Some of these may follow patterns shown in Figure 9.4.*

- Internal circulation with the uses arranged around the perimeter
- A hierarchical arrangement, beginning with less important uses leading to more important ones
- Tree-shaped form, branching off in linear arrangements

Obviously, some of the arrangements will lend themselves to your given site better than others. The object of the exercise

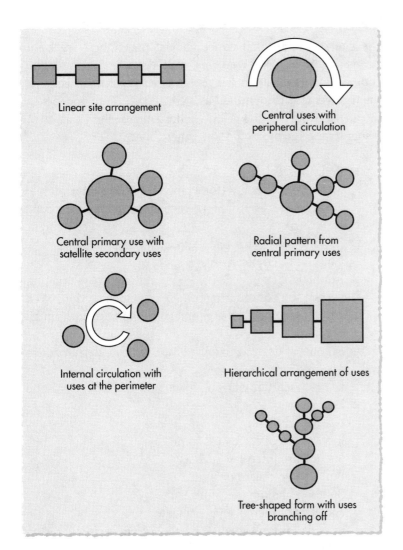

Linear site arrangement

Central uses with
peripheral circulation

Central primary use with
satellite secondary uses

Radial pattern from
central primary uses

Internal circulation with
uses at the perimeter

Hierarchical arrangement of uses

Tree-shaped form with uses
branching off

Figure 9.4   Examples of conceptual arrangements of site development patterns. Idealized bubble diagrams may follow these patterns or others. The patterns are modified when they are positioned on the site.

is to clarify the spatial relationships of the uses and linkages in the designer's mind. The bubble diagrams may cause the designer to do more research to satisfy his or her curiosity about what works and what doesn't. As designers mature, they often do some of this work subconsciously, especially if they've designed many of the same kinds of projects in the past. Bubble diagramming is still a worthwhile exercise and allows the designer to move to the ARS step with much greater ease and assurance.

Other Concept Types

The site organizational concepts just mentioned are by no means the only type of concepts. Indeed, some designers don't think of site organization as a design concept. In this book, spatial arrangement is identified as a concept. Other concepts can be put into play at the ARS, preliminary design, and detail design stages. Examples of these other concepts are:

- Philosophical:
  Metaphor or theme (for example: Man's evolution from an agrarian to a modern society, or the melting pot of cultures)
  Historic style (Victorian, Art Deco, rustic)
  Cultural or ethnic style
- Aesthetic
  Classic style or ordering principle (golden section, etc.)
  Parti (use of a simple geometric shape throughout the design)
  Schools of design thought (Beaux Arts, modern, contemporary, Prairie)
  Form-based (curvilinear, geometric)
- Ecological
  Natural, endemic
  Restoration of ecological community
- Site/feature interplay, such as:
  Building dominant on site
  Building blending into site
  Facilities hidden from entry view
  Secluded improvements separated from each other, etc.

THE SITE

Site Inventory

Besides the program of uses, the other starting point is the site. Most of us are attracted to the site; that's why we got into this business in the first place. We want to go there and spend time. We like to take photos and look for signs of wildlife or history. We like to observe the landform and feel the direction of the wind. The notion of site is very romantic and deeply ingrained in us.

When we first begin to work in an office, we are amazed to learn how little time is actually spent on the site and how much information comes from the city or county. It's not nearly as much fun to pore over utility maps as it is to crawl through the underbrush in a downpour. But we learn also to rely on photos and videos that remind us of the myriad details that exist on any site.

The site inventory is usually organized into physical (natural and built elements) and cultural (aesthetic and political) components. Here are some of the characteristics that we record about the site. The actual assortment will vary with the size, location, and scope of the project.

PHYSICAL (NATURAL AND BUILT)	CULTURAL (AESTHETIC AND POLITICAL)
Topography, landform	Parcel boundaries
Drainage patterns	Ownership
Soils	Land use (on and adjacent to the site)
Vegetation (overstory, groundcovers, etc.)	Zoning, overlay districts
Specimen trees	Easements, rights-of-way
Rock outcroppings	Views to and from the site
Bodies of water, springs	Jurisdictions (such as city, county, school district, water district, fire protection, etc.)
Microclimate (wind, temperatures)	
Utilities	Property values
Access (roads, public transit)	Odors
Hazards (landslides, faults)	Significant historical activity
Existing structures or buildings	Visual integrity

The paper and digital sources of these data types have been discussed in Chapter 5. Errors in recording or interpreting existing conditions that begin at this stage will multiply as we move through the process. This potential for expanding errors is why changes during construction are so bothersome and expensive. The designer must retrace many steps in order to correct even a minor error. Thus, it is worth the effort to double-check the information collected during the site inventory stage of the process.

Not the Sum of Its Parts

The site is a vital, living place; it is more than rock and soil and plants. Landform and tree cover combine to create space. Noisy streets and secluded valleys create contrast. Pleasing site proportions and a clear stream create beauty. The surrounding lands create views and context. It is these "composite conditions" that require human identification. (At this time, it is still difficult to write a program that would allow a computer to identify spatial quality or aesthetic conditions. With advances in expert systems, decision support systems, and/or neural networks, it may not always be so. See Chapter 11.)

If we prepared a composite map showing all the conditions at once, it would be unreadable. The site analysis must reduce the volume of information to an amount we can process at a glance. All the other information is still available to us; we just won't see it as part of the site analysis. Some conditions are more important to one project's program than they are to another's. Part of the site analysis process is to identify the hierarchy of conditions for the program at hand. For projects requiring large flat areas, such as parking lots, steep slopes are very important, whereas a retreat center may need more privacy and steep slopes are not such a detriment. So not only are some elements more important at different times, some of the same elements can be positive conditions for one set of uses and negative conditions for another. The designer's judgment is critical in determining the elements that will be visible in each site analysis.

The purpose of the site analysis is to serve as a guide for placement of the proposed facilities. Therefore, the site analysis selects those conditions that are most important to the program over the entire site. In some places on the site soils may be the most important condition because there isn't much else going on there. In other parts, it's not necessary to show soils because vegetative cover is more important.

The Big Picture

The site analysis identifies composite conditions and priority information. This analysis is not an inventory; it shows only those conditions that have been identified as being most important at each area of the site. The individual theme maps (soils, vegetation, slope analysis, etc.) are still available to the designer during the ARS and preliminary design if reference to them is needed.

Yes, to Scale

The site analysis is drawn to scale. Scale is necessary at the next stage, the ARS, so the designer will have the ability to determine whether there is enough room on the site for the proposed facilities or whether the program analysis should be reworked.

Site Analysis Is Not a Suitability Map

The site analysis does not suggest suitable locations for the proposed uses; the designer will do that at the ARS stage. The site analysis simply identifies the constraints and opportunities that exist because of the physical and cultural components. This differentiation between a site analysis and a suitability map is important. It is one of the reasons that GIS has not been accepted by some site designers, and it is one impetus for development of the GIS site analysis described in Chapter 10.

The Media Is the Message

Some site qualities may be represented as solid tones on the site analysis. These are usually areal conditions like soils, slope categories, or vegetation. Lines, such as roads and parcel boundaries, and other nonareal features, like buildings, can be drawn over the solid tones. Other conditions, like landform or viewsheds, can be illustrated over the solid tones with hatch patterns or strong, nearly parallel lines to indicate major escarpments or bluffs. Labels and short notes add qualifiers that can't be illustrated at this scale. Arrows can be used to show the direction of

North, the primary wind patterns, or major views. The site analysis is a complicated image, but very vital if the next step, the ARS, is to be successful.

THE AREA RELATIONSHIP STUDY

Try It On For Size

The purpose of the area relationship study (ARS) is to assign the various uses to their appropriate locations on the site. In many cases there are not many alternatives because all the usable parts of the site are filled up with program requirements. It then becomes a matter of switching locations or changing the forms of the proposed elements.

Assemble Your Earlier Products

In order to begin the ARS, the site designer brings the site analysis and several of the workable bubble diagrams together, as well as any site condition matrices that were prepared earlier.

Figure 9.5 The site analysis shows the constraints and opportunities available on the site. Whereas the inventory maps show each type of physical and cultural condition for the entire site, the site analysis shows only the most critical conditions.

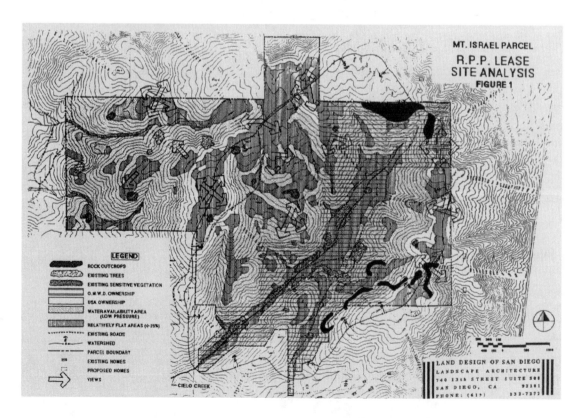

In order to give scale to the facilities, the program should include minimum, maximum, and optimum sizes for each element. The ARS is drawn with a scale in one hand and a pencil or marker in the other. Thus, the three previous work products (program matrices, bubble diagrams, and site analysis) are pulled together to prepare the ARS.

Tailoring the Alterations

The bubble diagrams may now need to be shifted, elongated, or broken into segments, or elements may need to be switched or rotated, in order to fit in the suitable zones on the site. This reordering takes some persistence and creativity.

Interdisciplinary Site Design

The design team for most projects includes several disciplines: usually a civil engineer, a landscape architect, and an architect. All should participate in the ARS. On ridgelines buildings and parking areas often become long and narrow, or portions go below grade or to a second level. On flat sites buildings may become multistory in order to gain height and views, or they may stretch out to be visually less obtrusive. With considerations of this type, it should be obvious that the design team's landscape architect, architect, and civil engineer should be working together. If several designers are working together, patience and mutual respect will be required; valid, sensitive site designs will be the result.

Select the Best

As with the idealized bubble diagrams, there may be a few acceptable ARSs. Tests can be applied to select the best one or two. Cross-sections should be generated, and preliminary cost estimates can be prepared. Reviews with other team members and the client can help in selecting the best ARS.

A presentation of the ARS to interest groups or citizens can sometimes be a useful exercise. The advantage of reviewing the ARS prior to the preliminary design is that the audience is forced to talk about big issues. They will not be distracted by design issues like sidewalk widths or plant materials selection. They are limited to talking about site layout topics: access, arrival experience, sequence of spaces, internal views, adequate parking. Design issues are important too, but site layout issues should be resolved first.

THE PRELIMINARY DESIGN

Form Givers

Once the site layout has been firmly established, the elements of finished landform, plants, and hardscape will take form. We continue to design with a scale in one hand, but we're also giving two-dimensional form to hardscape, water elements, and planting beds. We begin to suggest the third dimension with rough spot heights on retaining walls and by adjusting contours. We select materials and sketch details to go with the built elements. We're not calling out plant species, but we are suggesting their structural types: conical evergreen shrubs, overhead canopy trees, lawn. We may suggest color palettes for plants and pavements. Some designers cut photos out of maga-

Figure 9.6   The area relationship study (ARS) superimposes the bubble diagram on the site analysis. The ARS locates the uses in ways that take advantage of the site's characteristics while maintaining the spatial juxtapositions and linkages identified in the bubble diagrams.

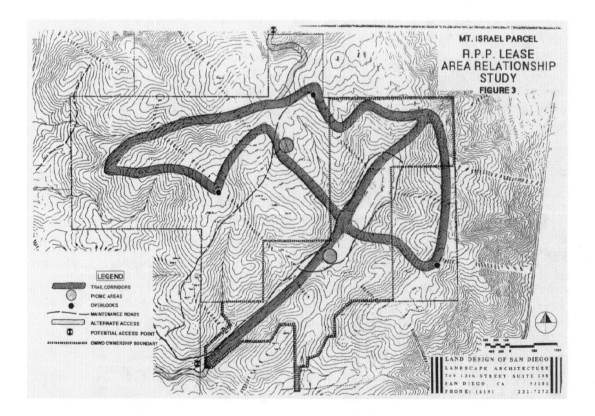

zines to illustrate the use of materials, the juxtaposition of design elements or textures, or the nuances of moving water. This step is where some people with native talent, and those who are not properly trained, begin. For the vast majority of site designers, preliminary design is near the end of an important process. Site design calls on experience and education and makes us valuable to our clients.

Great Designers: Born or Trained?

There are some designers who can take a piece of tracing paper and, without benefit of matrices or bubbles or even a thorough site analysis, can quickly sketch sound, intelligent, insightful site plans, time after time. There aren't many of them, though. Then there are those who cannot train themselves to follow a process, and occasionally they produce good designs. Many times, however, they work very hard at site plans, revising and modifying for hours, only to have the civil engineer say, "That won't work; my big storm drain is coming right through here. Didn't you look at my plans?" Then these designers go back to the drawing board more frustrated than ever.

The belief of most teachers is that motivated students can be made into designers. They will not be equally capable in the end; some do have more native talent than others, and some have the benefit of exposure through travel or the advantage of parents who encouraged early art lessons. A few will never get it. They cannot do site design, mainly because they will not accept the discipline of following a process. These undisciplined designers are the field observers and specification writers of tomorrow. But most students can be trained to be good designers. They need to build a repertoire of design precedents through readings, site visits, and classroom discussion, and they must allow themselves to follow a process. After several years their process may involve shortcuts or some steps may become subconscious, but in the beginning the full process must be followed if they are to learn to be creative and accountable designers.

Why Should I?

What does this have to do with the use of GIS in site design? Some designers have been able to get away without following a process. GIS is not so forgiving. The interface demands clear, step-by-step direction from the designer. Chapter 7 speculated that this may be one of the reasons not all designers are willing to test the GIS approach. Turn now to Chapter 10, and see if the approach described there is one you can work with.

REFERENCES

Koberg, Don, and Jim Bagnall. 1972. *The Universal Traveler.* Los Altos, CA: William Kaufmann. New Horizons Edition, 1991. Los Altos, CA: Crisp Publications.

SUGGESTED READING

Ching, Francis, D.K. 1996. *ArchitectureForm, Spatial and Order,* 2d ed. New York: Van Nostrand Reinhold.

Molnar, Donald, with Albert Rutledge. 1986. *Anatomy of a Park.* New York: McGraw-Hill.

Simonds, John O. 1961. *Landscape Architecture: The Shaping of Man's Natural Environment.* New York: McGraw-Hill.

10

A GIS'er in Disguise As a Site Designer: Step by Step through the Digital Site Design Process

This chapter is the heart of this book: it is here that an innovation in GIS application will be documented. On its surface, this new technique may appear subtle, but if it can open the world of Geographic Information Systems to a new group of people, to those who are more designer than technologist, then it is worth consideration.

The process documented here uses GIS capability, other digital abilities, and digital data in some unorthodox ways—that is, if GIS in the 1990s is old enough to have orthodoxy! Parts of the process are still manual, but technologies are already being developed that may allow greater automation, if that is desirable. The design process in GIS will certainly continue to evolve. This process is the first step in a creative journey to integrate site designers into the larger realms of regional and urban planning, visual resource protection, and natural resource management.

The process described here follows the design process detailed in Chapter 9. If any of the terms or steps in this chapter are unclear, refer to that text.

Note: All the maps and diagrams shown in this book are in gray tones. The accompanying CD shows most of these images, and others, in color.

GOALS, OBJECTIVES, AND PROGRAMS

If the goal is the ultimate result, the objectives define the routes to be taken to achieve the goal and the program specifies the uses and facilities that will give life to those objectives. This discussion will center on goals, objectives, and programs that are developed in verbal and written formats, without the benefit of digital information. However, we should not jump to the conclusion that no digital data is involved in this decision making. So much information now resides in databases that if feasibility studies or revenue projections have been generated for the project, it is likely that databases were consulted. They may not currently be associated with the spatial operators available in a GIS, but as digital data, the database records have potential to become part of a GIS.

PROGRAM ANALYSIS

The two halves of the program analysis, both decision matrices and bubble diagrams, can easily be represented using computer programs. Spreadsheet applications produce great-looking, easy-to-update matrices. Simple drawing programs are sophisticated enough to produce the spatial relationships shown in bubble diagrams. Examples of both of these are shown here. At this time the execution of these interim products is, in fact, manual, but with computer output. The potential exists to make matrix assignments based on database queries, but that synthesis has not yet been attempted by these authors.

SITE INVENTORY

As digital data, the site's physical and cultural inventory may be obtained from sources identified in Chapter 5. These data types include topography, roads, bodies of water, political boundaries, and land use and they are available in a variety of formats. In urban areas great amounts of data exist in CADD format, most of which can be imported to the GIS. CADD data is usually at a very fine resolution and includes themes such as utilities, streets, curbs, and property lines; however, it does not include attribute tables or topology. (*Note:* If you are not reading this

HONEY SPRINGS BATTLEFIELD PARK						
Matrices suggest correlations of proposed uses with certain existing natural and cultural conditions. These charts become guidelines in the design process.						

USE MATRIX: Natural Conditions

SITE CONDITION ⟶ PROPOSED USE: ⟶	Flood zone	Tree canopy	Steep slope			
Protection zones	OK	OK	OK			
Interpretive zones, trails	OK	OK, good	Not good			
Hiking trails	OK	OK, good	Not good			
Visitor info center (V.I.C.)	Not allowed	OK	Not good			
Parking	Not good	OK	Not good			
Maintenance facility	Not allowed	OK	Not good			
Small picnic areas	Not good	OK, good	Not good			

USE MATRIX: Cultural Conditions

SITE CONDITION ⟶ PROPOSED USE: ⟶	Ownership	Historic land	Visual qual.			
Protection zones	Public best, private w/easem't OK	Required	Important			
Interpretive zones, trails	Same	OK, not req'd	Very important			
Hiking trails	Public best	Not req'd	Important			
Visitor info center (V.I.C.)	Public req'd	Not req'd	Very important			
Parking	Public best	Not req'd	Important			
Maintenance facility	Public req'd	Best if not	Unimportant			
Small picnic areas	Public best	Best if not	Very important			

Figure 10.1 Matrices can be part of the program analysis. Decision matrices can be used to select program elements (see Figure 9.2). The matrices here document which site conditions are desirable for each use and which are not.

book from front to back, you may have to review Chapters 4 and 6 to acquaint yourself with some of the basic GIS terminology and concepts used in this chapter.)

Because CADD is developing greater links to GIS, virtually any new CADD data can be imported into the GIS environment. Data can also be input with advanced, simple-to-use digitizers and miraculously simple scanners. So, site inventory is still a process of collecting and evaluating the quality of physical and cultural themes. The beauty of GIS is that data from many diverse sources, with a wide variety of attributes and map symbols, can be brought together in a single medium where everything can be viewed at the same size, perfectly aligned, and with a consistent palette of symbols, patterns, and colors.

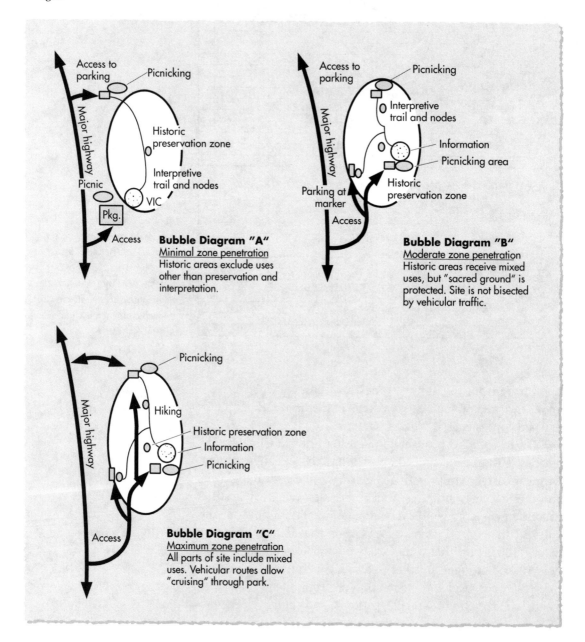

Bubble Diagram "A"
<u>Minimal zone penetration</u>
Historic areas exclude uses other than preservation and interpretation.

Bubble Diagram "B"
<u>Moderate zone penetration</u>
Historic areas receive mixed uses, but "sacred ground" is protected. Site is not bisected by vehicular traffic.

Bubble Diagram "C"
<u>Maximum zone penetration</u>
All parts of site include mixed uses. Vehicular routes allow "cruising" through park.

A Not-So-Different Site Analysis

The final site analysis image will be quite comparable to that which site designers have produced by hand for many decades. The GIS-produced site analysis is still more like that manual method than like the McHarg suitability model (reviewed in Chapter 6). It has output that is significantly similar to a manually produced site analysis: all the important information is shown in graphic representations, not as numeric values or in graduated tonal representations. This site analysis has symbols, patterns, tones, and labels that can be identified in a simple legend. It will be readable by the lay person and the designer without additional explanation.

Here We Go: The GIS Site Analysis

We now begin to prepare a site analysis in a GIS environment. Like the site design process described in Chapter 9, this site analysis will make judgments about those conditions that are important to the program at hand. In order to give the computer the instructions it needs to prepare this document, we will follow a series of seven steps.

STEP ONE: SELECT RELEVANT AREAL THEMES

Depending on the program and the site, certain themes may not be relevant to a given project. The school district within which a retail outlet sits has little effect on the spatial design of its site; a rural site may have no zoning. Some urban sites, especially for redevelopment projects, may have no vegetation worth including in the analysis, whereas the vegetation on most sites is extremely important.

SELECT ONLY NECESSARY THEMES FOR VISUAL CLARITY

The total number of themes will vary; a good guide for legibility of the site analysis is five to ten total areal themes. The most frequently used areal themes include soils, slopes, vegetation, ownership, floodways, viewsheds, zoning types, land use, historic zones, and aspect. Some of these themes may be split into two or more themes, based on program requirements. This multiple assignment is demonstrated in Step Two, in regard to binary maps.

Note that none of the linear or point elements are included here, because they can be shown over the areal information and need not be involved in the first part of this mapping exercise. The outcome of this exercise will not be meaningful numeric values, but rather an image that is intrinsically, visually meaningful.

STEP TWO: MAKE EACH THEME BINARY

In this context, *binary* means that only two conditions exist in an "either/or" juxtaposition. In digital terms, *binary* means that a value of 0 or a value of 1 are the only options. As far as the thematic maps are concerned, you will make assignments of

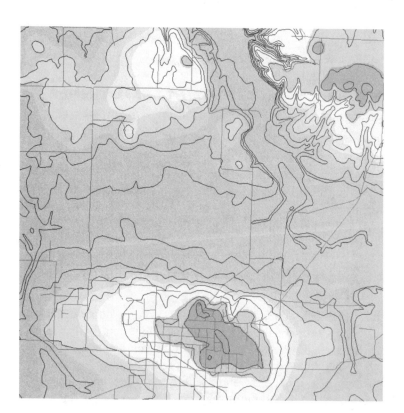

Figure 10.3 One of the most important layers of site information is the elevation model. This is a digital elevation model (DEM) with contour lines and county roads overlaid.

"yes" or "no" based on the ability of a given attribute to accommodate or affect the proposed uses.

Describe Appropriateness in Binary Terms

Consider this example. A regional park with proposed day and overnight uses will need rest room facilities. If the park is not very near to a sewage treatment facility, it may require septic systems. One might then look at each soil type on the site in terms of its septic system capacity, usually expressed as percolation rate. The county soils report, which accompanies the soils maps, will tell which soils are acceptable for septic systems and which are not. The designer then makes a list of the acceptable soils and reclasses all the soils. (If you need to refresh your memory on the "reclass" operator, see Chapter 6.)

All soils will be listed as acceptable or unacceptable. The computer will call up a list of all the soils, and you will designate each as "yes" or "no" by giving a value of 1 to the "yes" soil

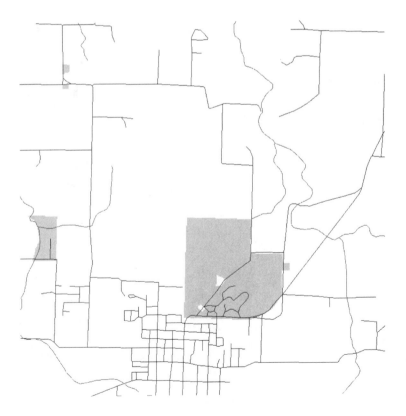

Figure 10.4 This public ownership map has relevance to site planning decisions.

types and a 0 to the "no" types. When the reclassed map is displayed, there will be only one color, showing the combined areas of all the "yes" (or 1) soil types and a background of white (or black) representing the "no" (or 0) types. In other words, you will see only the soil types that satisfy the condition "acceptable for septic systems."

One Theme Can Become Multiple Binary Maps

This step need not be the end of the soils considerations. Another binary map can be generated from the same basic theme, showing those soils with or without satisfactory structural conditions for building, or with excessive shrink/swell or erosion potential, or with agricultural fertility characteristics. In other words, each theme need not be reduced to a single map. There may be several facets of the information that are represented on separate maps, but each interim theme must show only a binary set of conditions for this GIS process to work.

Figure 10.5 A raster map of soils in the study area, showing all existing types. Each type is listed as an "attribute" in the associated database.

Figure 10.6   The soils have now been reclassed into a binary map showing suitable soils for septic systems.

POSITIVE OR NEGATIVE CONDITIONS NEED NOT PERMEATE THE PROCESS

Notice that the conditions shown do not have to be all positive or all negative. The goal is to design the map to be easily read. If it makes sense to show tree canopy as a readable binary condition and non-tree-canopy as white space on the map, the trees need not represent a positive or negative condition. Just as with a manual site analysis, the tree canopy simply exists and becomes part of our integrated evaluation. In this regard this method differs greatly from McHarg suitability maps, where all conditions must be either positive or negative in terms of their development suitability. This requirement can limit creativity, to say nothing of the confusion it often causes with lay audiences.

Keep Flexible

Another advantage of working in a GIS is that if the composite site analysis map does not reflect the information you need to do your design, it is very easy to adjust the binary maps. If field investigation shows that the reclass exercise has an error in an attribute rating, and a condition originally listed as "important to this activity" is, in fact, "not important," then adjust the binary map. GIS should not make one a slave to the digital domain; it is a tool that serves the designer's purpose. The important precaution is to continually question your own actions and the computer's output. Just because the computer is doing much of the work, it doesn't mean that we should abandon our role of asking questions.

STEP THREE: RANK THE THEMES

The purpose of this step is to set the visual hierarchy of the site analysis map. It is exactly the same step you would follow if you were manually preparing a site analysis map, although you may do the ranking subconsciously.

RANKINGS PRECEDE GRAPHIC HIERARCHY

We cannot show all the information across the entire site. We must extract from the total inventory those elements that will be most useful in the design procedure. In this GIS technique we achieve graphic hierarchy in several steps, the first of which is ranking the themes.

The themes may be ranked either according to their importance to a particular program or by the difficulty in replacing or overcoming them in the development. For instance, here is a list of considerations for developing rank order, followed by their assigned rankings.

> *Impermeable soils* Requirement(s) to overcome: Excavate and replace with permeable soils, or, if possible, extend connection to existing sewage treatment system. Ranking is low.

Steep slopes   Requirements to overcome: Additional grading, which may result in more visible cut or fill slopes; installation of retaining walls if necessary. Ranking is moderate to low.

Private ownership   Requirements to overcome: Purchase of property or purchase of conservation easement. In extreme conditions, eminent domain action. Ranking is moderate to high.

Mature trees   Requirements to overcome: Replacement of mature trees would require at least 25 years of growth (in these climate and soil conditions). Ranking is high.

Floodways   Requirements to overcome: In some cases levees can be built, but this option can be costly or uncertain. The risk of failure is replacement of built elements such as buildings, playgrounds, ballfields, etc., and possible loss of life. Ranking is very high.

The ranking established for this set of themes is:

- Lowest: impermeable soils
- Next highest: steep slopes
- Next highest: private ownership
- Next highest: mature trees
- Highest: floodways

This ranking reflects the condition that will be seen in each spot on the composite site analysis. If the only mapped condition that exists in a given location is impermeable soils, that is the condition that will read in that area. If the most critical condition is mature trees, that is the condition that will be visible in that location. The information about what else exists in each location is still available by querying the associated database, even when these other conditions are not seen on the site analysis map. If you think that some other condition, such as a viewshed, should also be seen, that can be displayed as an overlaid pattern, as we will discuss in Step Six.

The establishment of the rankings can be subjective, but most design judgments are subjective in some ways. Even in the McHarg method, the assignment of suitability values can be quite subjective. One of the dangers of computerized work is that many people do not realize that the input and the choice of operators is made by people. To be sure, these are trained professionals, but be aware that digital maps can be just as fallible as manually prepared maps. As illustrated in Chapter 8, the public seems to trust the accuracy and recommendations of computer-generated maps more than hand-drawn maps. The design team must never forget "GIGO" (garbage in = garbage out).

STEP FOUR: ASSIGN PLACEHOLDER VALUES AND SUM THE OVERLAYS

This process is fundamentally different from the McHarg suitability method. It gives the designer a much more intuitive product with which to work. The site analysis allows the designer to use traditional thought processes and to retain more control over the information.

CLASSIC MCHARG OVERLAYS

Any of us who has prepared McHarg overlays with shaded film on acetate knows that each data attribute (category) receives its own numeric value, which is visually represented by an assigned degree of darkness. For instance, if, for a historical preservation project, mature trees are assigned a value of 10 and disturbed grassy areas receive a value of 1, then the areas assigned a 10 will be much darker than those areas receiving the value of 1. There is a direct correlation between the assigned value and the darkness of the shaded film applied to the acetate. If there is another theme called "existing land use," those areas that are undeveloped may receive a high preservation value (and a dark tone), whereas those covered with buildings may receive a low value and a light tone. When all the values are superimposed, the darkest composite areas will have the greatest preservation value and the lightest will have the lowest value. This shading is fairly straightforward and has been used as the basis for many planning studies. This process has quite readily been taken into the GIS domain, where it has been widely applied and accepted.

In order to make the distinction between McHarg acetate overlays and their digital equivalent, the term *suitability map* will be applied to the computerized version. This discussion will now refer to all summed digital overlays of McHarg valued themes as suitability maps. The new method being described will be called the GIS graphic method.

Suitability Map Evaluation

One criticism of the original McHarg acetate and shading method is that it sometimes becomes difficult to discern relative darkness and lightness across the surface of the composite map. This lack of clarity has been corrected in the digital environment, where an accurate numeric sum is available at each point on the map. Visually, the computer also compensates with a very broad array of gray tones, good screen resolution, and improved output devices that produce clear, legible graphics.

Another criticism of the McHarg acetate method is that the assignment of values obscures the visual form of existing conditions: the visual clues that we rely on to conduct our design work are absorbed in the value assignments. This problem is in part a result of the requirement that each condition be positive or negative, not merely existing.

A third criticism, in regard to suitability maps, is that once the thematic values have been summed, it becomes very difficult to determine exactly which attribute components were involved in yielding those sums on a point-by-point basis.

Why Placeholder Values?

A special system of value assignment is proposed here which overcomes the second and third criticisms. It shows the important existing conditions without losing the outline of each condition on the map. In the suitability map method, the form of an existing condition is often lost as a result of the value assignments. With the GIS graphic method, the condition is allowed to retain most of its form so we can see where it occurs. This technique also allows the summed values to be unique: each composite value can represent only one set of conditions. Here is how it works.

ELIMINATE DUPLICATED SUMS

In a standard suitability analysis the value 1 will be assigned to one attribute on one theme, and to another attribute on another theme. The values 2, 3, and so on, will also be assigned to different conditions on different themes. When the assigned values are added together, unless one does very clumsy queries, there can be many combined conditions that equal 2 or 3 or 4 when added together. Observe:

1 for clay soils	1 for erosive soils
+1 for coastal scrub	+1 for objectionable views
2	**2**

1 for windy areas	
+2 for grasslands	
3	**3** for migrating fowl habitat

There are two flaws here: (1) You cannot tell whether the summed value includes one or more than one theme, and (2) identical summed values give no clue as to the constituent conditions that contributed to that sum.

PLACEHOLDERS MAKE IT DECIPHERABLE

With placeholder values, the numeric assignment has no inherent judgment attached to it, except for its rank. Here is how it works:

Value Assignments by Rank

RANK	THEME	ASSIGNED VALUE
Lowest	Permeable soils	1
Next highest	Steep slopes	2
Next highest	Private ownership	4
Next highest	Mature trees	8
Highest	Floodways	16

Notice that for each step up in rank, the value assigned to the binary condition doubles. Review the following sums and note that each sum can represent only one, unique set of conditions.

Constituent Conditions of Summed Values

SUMMED VALUE	INCLUDED BINARY CONDITIONS
1	Permeable soils (only)
2	Steep slopes (only)
3	Permeable soils and steep slopes
4	Private ownership (only)
5	Permeable soils and private ownership
6	Steep slopes and private ownership
7	Permeable soils, steep slopes, and private ownership
8	Mature trees (only)
	. . . and so forth to 31 (for 5 themes)

Each sum can be only one set of conditions.

THE COMPUTER OPERATOR IS AGAIN "RECLASS"

Just as the reclass operator was used to generate the individual, binary themes, it is used once more to change the binary 1 to the assigned value for each of these themes. The placeholder values are shown in the preceding chart "Value Assignments by Rank." In each case the binary value 1 is changed to 1, 2, 4, 8, 16, and so forth.

OVERLAY AND SUM THE VALUES

This step is a map algebra operation. This first sequence of steps is looking at areal conditions only (not points or lines). In the raster format, there is a one-to-one corre-

Figure 10.7 *Graphic method, Step Four: Assign placeholder values and sum all binary themes. This "map" shows the sum of those placeholder values assigned to the binary themes.*

lation of grid cells from theme to theme. It is a simple matter of adding all the assigned values for each set of overlaid cells. In the vector format, the polygons are first overlaid, and where the outlines are not coincident, smaller, new polygons will be created. One sum will represent the value for each entire polygon, including each of the newly created slivers.

STEP FIVE: RECOLOR FOR LEGIBILITY

The overlay of five themes results in the 31 summed values and colors (shades) that appear on this map. And even though each represents a unique set of conditions, it is still too difficult to read. The next step will reduce the 31 colors to 5, representing only the most critical condition in each location. Remember, the summed value and its component conditions are available with a single query, rather than the much more complicated queries required of standard suitability maps. The primary goal is to give us a site analysis image that we can comprehend visually, as we are used to doing. The reason you recolor and do not reclass is to keep those unique sums available for direct query of the site analysis image.

Figure 10.8 *Suitability map recolor scheme: The computer assigns tones or colors corresponding to each summed value, 30 in different shades in this example.*

RECOLOR CHART

MOST CRITICAL CONDITION	VALUES TO BE SHOWN BY A SINGLE COLOR	REPRE- SENTATIVE COLOR	(SHADE)
Permeable soils	1	Yellow	(10% gray)
Steep slopes	2, 3	Ochre	(20% gray)
Private ownership	4, 5, 6, 7	Light brown	(30% gray)
Mature trees	8, 9, 10, 11, 12, 13, 14, 15	Dark green	(40% gray)
Floodways	16, 17, 18, 19, 20, 21, 22, 23, 24, 25, 26, 27, 28, 29, 30, 31	Dark blue	(50% gray)

STEP SIX: FINISH THE MAP

ADD VECTORS TO GIVE SPATIAL REFERENCE, INFORMATION

The recolored (reshaded) map is nearly complete, and it is beginning to look like a traditional site analysis map. By overlaying roads and parcel boundaries, we can orient ourselves quite easily to locations on the site and to the scale of the map. Other vectors include utility lines and rivers, polygon outlines of zones such as overlay districts. These are a necessary part of a functional site analysis, as is the areal information we portrayed earlier, plus point data, labels, and legends.

POINTS GIVE VISUAL REFERENCES, VITAL DATA

Among the important elements for visual analysis are existing buildings. In a GIS these are often so small that they are represented as points. Yet they help us understand the existing conditions as we proceed with the next step of the area relationship study (ARS). Buildings are essential to any visual integrity studies. The mapped component of visual integrity may be shown as areal data, shown as an outline, or overlaid as a pattern on the site analysis image, as described in the following discussion.

Other mapped points include springs, mine entries, nodes such as traffic lights, and archaeological sites. These too can be critical to site design and should be shown. Most GISs will allow different point data to be represented with different symbols or small icons.

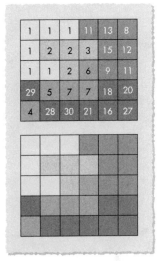

Figure 10.9   Graphic method, Step Five: Recolor. Shades of color added to particular ranges of values to make the image more readable. In each location only the most critical condition is visible. In the lower image, one can see from this tiny area how much more legible 5 shades are as compared with 30 shades, as shown in Figure 10.8. The information about all of the existing conditions is readily available in the summed values as shown in the upper image. Refer also to the Constituent Conditions chart.

PUT PATTERNS ON TOP

A second layer of areal information can be shown as patterns over the composite themes built in Steps One through Five. A common use of the pattern overlay is to show an important theme that covers much of the study area. If it has a high rank and is factored into the process, it will hide much of the other information. However, as a pattern overlay, it can still allow us to read the color polygons, vectors, and points beneath it. The translucent quality of the pattern overlay adds visual richness to the image while displaying additional spatial information. As many as three or four simple patterns can be applied and comprehended on the site analysis. This option raises the number of visually available themes from 5 or 10 to 9 or 14.

Cartographic Conventions

To complete the map, we need to add a title, the name(s) of study author(s) or agency, a North arrow, labels, borders, and legends. A bar scale is much more meaningful than a written scale or ratio, because digital maps are likely to be printed at a variety of scales. Sometimes the maps are printed to fill a certain size page, and the scale is not a standard one. Unusual scales are not such a burden in a GIS, because the computer can be used to take measurements and calculate areas and volumes. An odd scale is very cumbersome in trying to use an engineer's scale for measuring, but accurate calculations are easy within a GIS regardless of the size of the map.

STEP SEVEN: FINE-TUNING FOR MAXIMUM LEGIBILITY, FLEXIBILITY

Just as it is easy to switch the "shown/not shown" relationship of the binary themes, the GIS allows for trial and error in the composite site analysis as well. The individual decisions of binary assignments and ranking may not be as important as the functionality of the resulting site analysis map. If you cannot see the information you need in order to design, then by all means, change the model so you have an image that serves your pur-

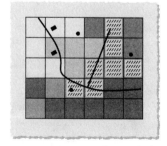

Figure 10.10   Graphic method, Step Six: Finish the map. After the site analysis map is recolored, various patterns, vectors, and point data can be superimposed on the areal data.

pose. The advantage of this method is that it allows you to use the intuitive approach that you have always used. Take advantage of the flexibility of GIS to give you the products you need to follow the procedure with which you are familiar and comfortable.

You may also use this site analysis as the base over which to display analyses by other design team members. The engineer may have completed a watershed analysis or alternate designs for impoundments. These can be imported and displayed over the site analysis image or as part of the site analysis. The biologist may have modeled several wildlife habitats, which can be displayed over the site analysis or incorporated as one of the initial themes. Because the image is showing these features as physical conditions, not as an evaluation, there is no need to review the assigned values in order to comprehend site conditions. What you see is what you get!

MODEL COMPARISONS

The following lists compare the steps used in the suitability map method with those used in the GIS graphic method.

Suitability map method

1. Select relevant themes.
2. Assign values to attributes based on their relative suitability for the given activity (or use). This value assignment is a reclass, based on the experience and judgment of the designer.
3. Determine weighting for each theme.
4. Use map algebra to overlay and combine the thematic values, multiply the values of the weighted themes, then add (or subtract) the resultant values for each area or grid cell.
5. Recolor (or shade) the combined overlays to correspond to the resultant total values.
6. Identify those areas with lightest tones as most (or least) suitable for the proposed use. Quantify acreages of each suitability class.

GIS graphic method

1. Select relevant areal themes.
2. Make them binary, based on importance to the proposed uses.
3. Rank the themes.
4. Assign placeholder values and sum the overlays.
5. Recolor to improve legibility.
6. Superimpose vectors, points, overlay patterns.
7. Modify as needed for maximum legibility. Quantify acreages of each visible, or invisible, condition as needed.

AREA RELATIONSHIP STUDIES

It can be argued that the suitability map method generates an area relationship study, as well as a site analysis. If that is true, it points to one of the reasons that the suitability map method has

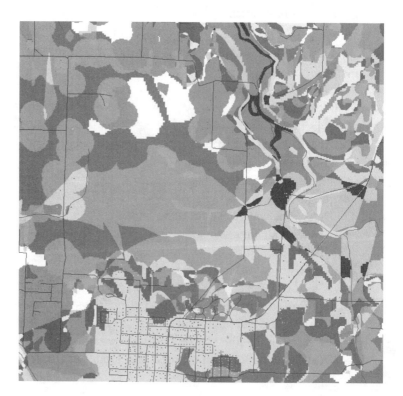

Figure 10.11 A standard suitability map with many colors and slivers, which make it very difficult to read.

Figure 10.12   Graphic method, Step Five: recolor. Here is the full image from which Figures 10.7 through 10.10 were clipped. Compare the legibility with that in Figure 10.11, which shows the suitability method. The graphic method is "direct read."

not been used widely for small-scale site design. It is inherently more useful at a regional scale and for studies leading to policies or zoning, or for broadly placed infrastructure such as roads or utility corridors. Projects that result in complicated site improvements are better served by the preparation of a true site analysis rather than, or in addition to, a suitability analysis.

FIT THE BUBBLE DIAGRAM ONTO THE SITE ANALYSIS

Because the site analysis is a visual tool, it can be "drawn on" the same way you would draw on a tracing paper overlay. This GIS site analysis is a "face value" document that will allow you to study the bubble diagrams and locate each use zone and linkage in a suitable place on the site, based on your judgment. This image making is exactly the way you would work with tracing paper and pencil, except now you will draw with a mouse or a computerized pen, either within the GIS or in a graphics program.

There will be several good ARSs, and maybe one or two exceptional ones. Just as when you are designing manually, it is your

Figure 10.13 Graphic method, Step Six: Finish the map. Here the pattern overlays represent important viewsheds and historically important zones. Vectors (lines) show roads and parcel boundaries. Homes, barns, and poultry houses have been added, as well as a legend, titles, bar scale, and North arrow.

challenge to consider many options, with several different spatial concepts and slight changes in shapes, in order to develop the most functionally valid, environmentally sensitive, aesthetically pleasing approach to a site design.

If this site analysis is used to incorporate the investigations of other design team members, those considerations can be made a part of alternate ARS schemes. These GIS products allow designers to access the power of digital data while using the methods they trust. This technique embraces both the logic of GIS and the creative pencil strokes of experienced designers.

Some GIS packages have freehand tools that allow you to work within that environment. Others are clumsy to use for several reasons:

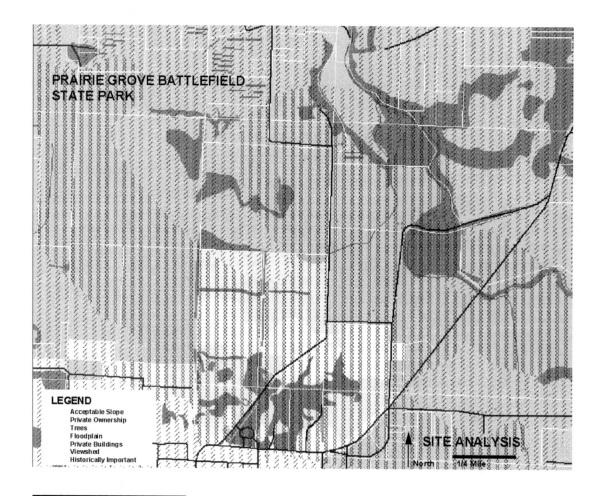

PRAIRIE GROVE BATTLEFIELD
STATE PARK

LEGEND
Acceptable Slope
Private Ownership
Trees
Floodplain
Private Buildings
Viewshed
Historically Important

SITE ANALYSIS

North   1/4 Mile

- Their "pencils" do not have shaping features, so smooth lines are difficult to draw
- The choices of line weights and styles are limited, so it is difficult to indicate conditions such as heavy versus light traffic patterns, vehicular versus pedestrian, and so forth
- The lines are so light they must be drawn as double lines, closing to make polygons that are then filled (closing these very long, narrow polygons—shaped like arrows—requires incredible repetitions of in and out zooms and lots of patience)

When your GIS package has these limitations, you can export the site analysis image to a graphics environment where you have many more symbol choices and fluid drawing tools. Be aware that when the image leaves the GIS environment, it is no longer interactive. It is no longer "smart," because it loses its database connectors. It retains its internal resolution and proportion, but it will no longer give you answers to data queries. This loss is not really a problem, because the original site analysis map is still saved in the GIS for later investigations.

Another option is to take the image into a CADD environment. This move will require a little more work, in terms of setting up scale, but if the ARS will ultimately be exported to CADD for design and construction documents, this will not be extra work. The advantage of taking the image into CADD is that as you work on the ARS, you can still have area, length, and perimeter calculations made for you by the program.

APPLY THE BUBBLE DIAGRAMS AS YOU ALWAYS HAVE: BY HAND

As you draw the use bubbles onto the site analysis, refer to those descriptive matrices you prepared earlier that point to the best characteristics for each activity. Priority will go to the more important uses; usually, the support uses are assigned to the parts of the site with less desirable characteristics. Your program should include minimum area requirements, and when you are drawing in the GIS environment or in a CADD environment, the computer can give you these calculations as you work.

Aerial Photos Make a Great Image Base

Once you have completed an exhaustive series of ARSs and have selected your preferred site plan, you now have an option that will make the ARS extremely easy to read, especially by citizens groups. In the course of setting up a GIS, one graphic image that is very useful is a recent aerial photo. This visual aid is good for comparing the accuracy of streets and roads, for actually developing your own vegetation theme, for verifying land use, and for other fact-finding exercises. But this visual confirmation is not the end of an aerial photo's usefulness. Although we have meticulously assembled the site analysis image, and although it allows us to use our familiar design

Figure 10.14   The area relationship study results when the bubble diagram is fitted to the site analysis. Even though this application is done in the computer, it is directed by the designer.

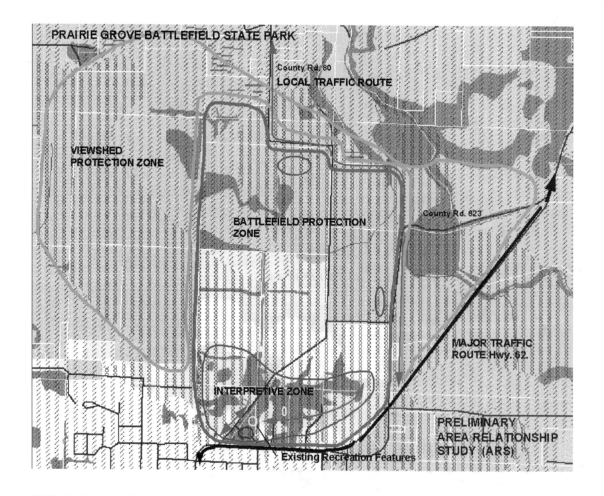

PRAIRIE GROVE BATTLEFIELD STATE PARK

County Rd. 80
LOCAL TRAFFIC ROUTE

VIEWSHED
PROTECTION ZONE

County Rd. 623

BATTLEFIELD PROTECTION
ZONE

MAJOR TRAFFIC
ROUTE Hwy. 62.

INTERPRETIVE ZONE

PRELIMINARY
AREA RELATIONSHIP
STUDY (ARS)

Existing Recreation Features

approach, once it has bubble outlines and circulation arrows drawn on it, it too can become visually cluttered.

One of the images we have developed is a "tint" of the ARS bubbles, superimposed on a black-and-white aerial photo. The outlined bubbles are converted to solid polygons, which eliminate the perimeter lines. The bubble itself is given a pale, translucent tint that designates the area of a particular use or activity while allowing the photo image to show through. (Unfortunately, in gray tones the tinted image disappears, so Figure 10.15 in this book is not a good example. Look at this same figure on the CD for its full effect.) The arrows indicating circulation patterns need not be transparent because they are so

Figure 10.15 The tinted bubble diagram is overlaid on the black-and-white photograph for clear communication of the development concepts.

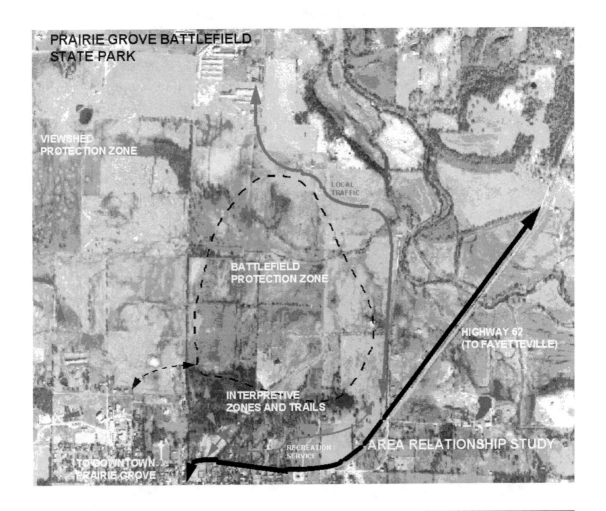

narrow. The resulting image allows people to see how the bubbles relate to roads, rivers, groups of trees, and existing buildings. It allows the people who live in the study area to visualize the proposal in spatial terms they can understand. Sometimes it shows the designer an overlooked condition that points to a flaw in the ARS. In this regard, the tint-photo-overlay becomes a fail-safe device, not just a great communication tool.

Three-Dimensional Drapes: More Computer Magic

One of the unique operators in most GIS packages is the three-dimensional terrain model. The operator allows you to select a viewpoint based on its:

- Height above a specified point in the study area
- Direction of view to the site
- Ratio of horizontal to vertical exaggeration of the ground plane
- Cone of vision (horizontal and vertical)

This tool allows the designer to familiarize him- or herself with the site in a rather exciting way. It's a lot cheaper and less scary

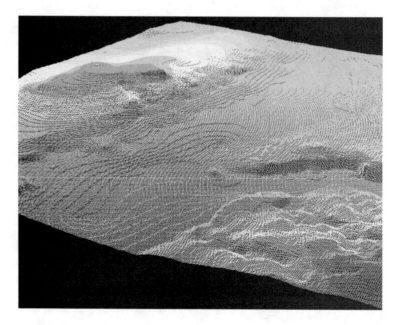

Figure 10.16 Computer terrain model—plain 3-D drape.

than a ride in a small plane. What's more, any theme can be used as the information displayed on the surface of the terrain model. This superimposition of a map image means that contours can be displayed or that the site analysis, or an aerial photo, or the ARS photo tint can be displayed over the terrain model. It is this last image that has been very successful in conveying to agency chiefs, other design team members, and the local public the essence of the proposal.

ARS on Photo Draped Over 3-D Terrain Model

The photo over the terrain model gives many visual references. Because it is in three dimensions, many people who struggle to understand maps can comprehend the relationships between proposals and physical landmarks. The ARS, when represented as a tint overlaid on the photo, is unmistakable. It is realistic and comprehensible even to the graphically uninitiated. These images never cease to be the topic of conversation.

Figure 10.17 The ARS over the black-and-white photograph can be draped over a digital terrain model to visualize the site in three dimensions.

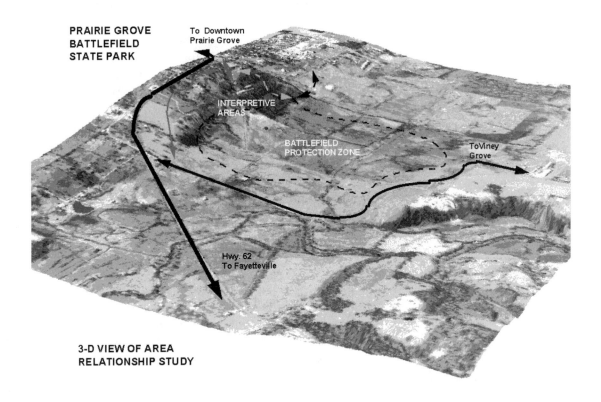

PRAIRIE GROVE
BATTLEFIELD
STATE PARK

To Downtown
Prairie Grove

INTERPRETIVE
AREAS

BATTLEFIELD
PROTECTION ZONE

To Viney
Grove

Hwy. 62
To Fayetteville

3-D VIEW OF AREA
RELATIONSHIP STUDY

Line It Up

Remember that if you take the site analysis image out of the GIS environment in order to draw the ARS on it, it is no longer interactive. When you reimport the ARS image, you must once more geo-reference it to the projection and rectify it to the grid originally used for all the basic themes. These adjustments are required so you can align the circulation arrows and bubbles and the photo features with their actual spatial locations. This step is also necessary so that these features will be accurately draped over the terrain model.

PRELIMINARY DESIGN

Here's where CADD becomes the more appropriate technology. The ARS is still not a preliminary design. It is a site plan, but the proposed facilities have not yet taken shape. Exact form must be given to roadway alignments, sidewalks, plazas, building foot-prints, parking areas, detention ponds, planting beds, retaining walls, and other improvements. A CADD environment is a good place to establish form for several reasons:

- The locations for circulation routes and use areas will be accurately transferred from the ARS to the design.
- The drawing tools in CADD are very advanced and relatively easy to use.
- Measurements can be taken that aid in decision making. If you need to know whether the turning radius on an emergency access road is adequate, the CADD system can give an accurate measurement quite readily. If you need to double-check the parking acreage in multiple lots, the CADD calculations are quick and simple.
- It is easy to save options on different layers. Thus, you can print out several options separately or superimpose two or more options on one print.
- Some CADD packages will generate cross-sections. The example shown in Figure 10.18 took a cross-section through one of the viewing points previously used to calculate a viewshed in the GIS. The cross-section from the viewpoint to a visual disturbance gave the detail needed to decide the proper height for a screening ele-

ment. A row of trees alone would not have adequately screened the off-site uphill intrusion; trees on top of an earth berm were needed to reach the desired height in a reasonable length of time.

■ Some CADD options, such as LandCADD, will give earthwork quantities to further enhance decision making during preliminary design.

Design Testing

The preliminary designs must then be tested through cost estimates, review of the third dimension (sections, perspectives, and elevations), client and/or public review, and possible environmental review. CADD tools assist in these tests and in preparing images to share with clients, public groups, or environmental consultants. The move to GIS does not terminate or diminish the designer's use of CADD. The two technologies

Figure 10.18 Cross-sections generated in the GIS, then exported to a CADD software package, were used to determine the height of screening elements.

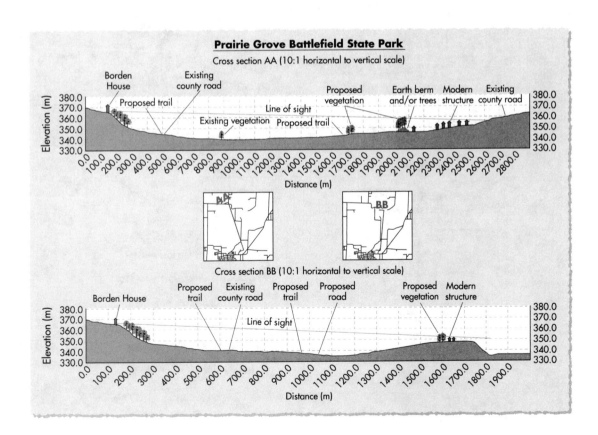

Figure 10.19   The final CADD drawings for the plan can be created using the base information developed within the Geographic Information System.

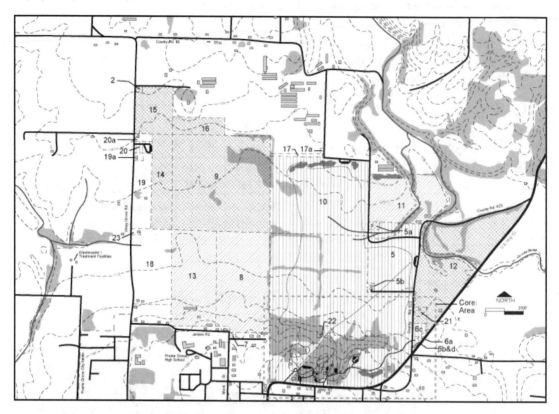

Prairie Grove Battlefield State Park

**Proposed Master Plan:
Phase Two**

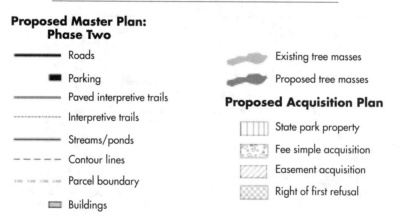

──────── Roads

▄▄▄ Parking

──────── Paved interpretive trails

·········· Interpretive trails

──────── Streams/ponds

─ ─ ─ ─ ─ Contour lines

╍ ╍ ╍ ╍ Parcel boundary

▭ Buildings

〰〰 Existing tree masses

〰〰 Proposed tree masses

Proposed Acquisition Plan

▦ State park property

▨ Fee simple acquisition

▨ Easement acquisition

▨ Right of first refusal

enhance each other and are quickly becoming a single type of application.

CONCLUSION

Is this designer's process less scientific or technical than other GIS models? The site analysis portion is no less rigorous than the suitability maps that preceded it. The designer still makes informed decisions about binary conditions, rankings, and visual output.

In this generation of the GIS site design process, the area relationship study is still somewhat subjective. Subjective decisions are a varying portion of all creative process, whether scientific hypothesis or design approach. Planners and designers make decisions based on their education and experience; some of those decisions may be subjective, but they are not arbitrary. Projects conducted in the realms of GIS and CADD can give the designer much more hard information with which to make creative decisions. The GIS environment allows the designer to examine the work of related disciplines in much closer context to his or her own analysis. The GIS graphic process presented here allows the site designer to work confidently in a manner to which he or she is accustomed. Among the design professions, the role of the site designer is critical to the genuine protection and sustainable enhancement of the built and natural environments.

SUGGESTED READING

McHarg, Ian. [1969] 1994. *Design with Nature*. New York: John Wiley & Sons.

PART FIVE

WHAT'S NEXT? IS THE NEW WORLD TRULY BRAVE?

The rate of change is never constant. Computer technology and digital media are currently undergoing very rapid changes. There is no reason to think that the design and construction industries will not be further affected. CADD has meant major changes in work products, work habits, personnel, office layout, capital investment, and marketing. Land planning and environmental assessment firms have seen their digital domains expand to include databases, GIS, and spatial modeling.

For the most part, site designers have embraced CADD, but they are falling behind the engineers and some planners in their reluctance to take the next logical step by using GIS. Many forces are at work generating better data sources, user-friendly computers and programs, and less expensive equipment. All indications are for the expansion and transparency of Geographic Information Systems. You owe it to yourself, at least, to be informed about their potential.

11

Our World Becomes
Ever More Digital

Our lives are already digital. We play CDs instead of LPs, components in our cars are computer controlled, all media now pass through a digital state, and some information is received as bits, not atoms. This trend will continue and broaden, for several reasons.

- It is far less expensive to put information, commands, and entertainment products in a digital form.
- Far fewer resources are consumed with digital information: fewer trees are cut for paper pulp; paper, plastics, and vinyl can be replaced by digital feed for newspapers, magazines, books, videos, CDs, and photographs. Storage space is incredibly reduced.
- Our private lives demand protection, not just privacy but freedom from invasion of our private time. Time has become so precious that we need to protect what personal time we have. E-mail currently is, and soon television and other media will be, delivered "on demand." Being "time asynchronous" offers the advantage of having messages delivered when we are ready for them; we don't have to communicate with someone simultaneously unless we choose to (Negroponte 1995, 167).

We will have few choices about "going digital." In this country, communications are controlled at the federal level, in close cooperation with the major suppliers. Media delivery systems will become more digital in response to changes in technology, public demand for quality and flexibility, and the market's demand for profit. Being digital is not just a trend; it is inevitable. Its effect on land planning and site design will be broad and pervasive. We will receive data in digital form, we will act on it in a digital environment, and interactive displays will increasingly replace static output.

DIGITAL CONSTRUCTION SITES

It is not so outrageous to imagine construction documents developed with "hypercard" software, viewed in the field on a laptop computer. Nodes on the plan views could be connected to details, specs, catalog cuts, sample photos, and even video clips. Hard copies could be produced for construction workers, or perhaps their hard hats could be equipped with tiny monitors and speakers that would remind them of spacing, dimensions, and fittings. These hard hats might be part of a remote local area network, with a base station in the construction trailer sending signals to them like a remote telephone handset. It may be less effort for workers to call up a drawing using their wrist-button-pad than to locate and search through a roll of tattered and mud-streaked blueprints. Updated drawings would be instantly available, and there would be no confusion over who has the latest set.

Shop drawings can already be sent to fabricators via the Internet. Remote video could be sent from the field to the design office to solve problems interactively, thus saving travel time and reducing work delays. Being digital is with us now, and its influence will only increase.

WHAT DOES "DIGITAL" MEAN TO SITE DESIGNERS?

Let us recap some recent advances in computer technology and their impact on planning and site design. Then we will move to some of the more interesting predictions about our digital world and their implications to the design professions.

First, let us disregard digital delivery of data and GIS applications in site design and focus on CADD and its impact. Not only has CADD increased the ease of modifications, scale changes, production of multiple, color-rendered drawings, and incorporation of interdisciplinary data, it has also improved our assessment of the third dimension. In the manual realm, two-dimensional maps and plans are always accompanied by sections, elevations, and perspectives. The need to portray the third dimension has always been crucial to exploring our ideas and explaining them to others.

RENDERERS HAVE BEEN DIGITAL

The need for three-dimensional images has been so great that small firms and individuals who specialize in perspective drawings are in very high demand. Once called "renderers," these professionals have long embraced the computer because it helps them generate more accurate perspective views: finer, more controlled lines can be generated, the size of an image can be modified, more alternatives of detail and color can be generated much more quickly, and different lighting effects can be applied with ease. Some projects demand this level of sophistication for presentations, publications, and funding decisions, and design professionals still use these outside consultants for complicated, presentation graphics, such as for major buildings, large campuses, and elaborate urban spaces.

EXPERIMENTING IN THE THIRD DIMENSION

However, the simpler drawings, especially those used to explore design alternatives, are mostly done in-house using three-dimensional components of CADD packages or other software into which we import CADD plans. This capacity to see the third dimension accurately and in many alternative views has improved our ability to criticize our own work, and if we use it properly, it improves our designs. Some people use the computer to generate a wire frame, over which they draw the design components, plants, cars, and people by hand (Thompson 1996, 41). Many clip art files exist for generating realistic elevations and perspectives by computer. Three-dimensional drawing packages are quite common and reasonably priced.

GIS Portrays Ground Planes

In a GIS a three-dimensional product can be generated that is very difficult to attain in CADD: a terrain model. Contours present unique difficulties to most CADD and some GIS applications. In these settings contours are seen as lines, or vectors, each representing a constant set of values (equal elevation). The area between the contours is usually perceived as being flat, taking on the elevation of the lower contour. This misconception results in a "terraced" effect: the computer thinks the ground plane steps up in terraces equal to the contour interval.

Advanced GIS applications interpolate between the contours and represent the ground plane as it really is, at least to the extent of the resolution of the contour information. In other words, if the contours are at an appropriate interval (for instance, 1-foot contours in a relatively flat area, or 20- or 50-foot contours in mountainous areas), then the GIS can represent the ground plane with a realistic image. As explained in Chapter 6, this terrain model can be generated from any height or angle, with any exaggeration of the horizontal to vertical ratio. So far, I've described qualities that can be done manually, yet with much difficulty. Not only can the GIS produce these images, but many alternative views can be shown and virtually any proposal can be superimposed to give a three-dimensional view at bird's-eye or passerby elevation. This terrain drape operation will become a common feature of planning and site design projects. It is already available, but it is not yet being used to its full capacity.

VISUALIZE THIS!

Another capacity that has not yet been fully explored is data visualization. Such images can be generated on a flat map, placed in perspective view with roads, parcel lines, and other features superimposed, or shown on a terrain model. The image itself shows numbers, vertical bar graphs, icons of various sizes, and/or labels that translate information from the database into a map showing the incidence of occurrences in their correct geographic locations.

If, for instance, a database included the numbers of people who worked in each building in an urban area and their work times, this data could be represented in 3-D map form for critical hours, such as arrival and departure times. This map would be a very useful graphic in designing parking facilities or in locating mass transit stops. A typical design objective is to minimize conflicts between major pedestrian access to mass transit and vehicular traffic at major parking sites. If the numbers of people and their destinations were mapped, the choreography of this urban dynamic could be supported by precise information, rather than just an educated guess.

Good Data Supports Good Decisions

Data visualization will expand as databases are compiled to supply the requisite information for decision making. Perhaps a commercial census will be added to our decennial residential census. Traffic counts might be able to classify vehicles by length or weight, in addition to numbers, thus generating a more accurate ratio of full-size to compact cars. Counts of bicycles, motorcycles, and pedestrians would improve the ability of planners and designers to make decisions about origins and destinations. There are many firms in the business of collecting data for use by retailers, franchisees, advertisers, and mail order companies. If the demand existed for other types of data, the data would appear (Mapping Science Committee 1993), either through government agencies, data vendors, or freelancers who collect data on an "as needed" basis.

REMOTELY SENSED DATA: TECHNOLOGY IN THE SKY

This book has not yet addressed remote sensing. Generally, the two types of data collected by "remote sensors" are radar and satellite imagery. Radar images are generated from the reflection of radio waves, and the resulting images resemble photographs. Satellites collect data that are transmitted back to earth based on the reflective qualities of light. Four commonly collected data types from satellites show:

Wetness	Greenness
Brightness	Thermal capacity

These are very sophisticated systems, and one of the limitations encountered in using them is the tremendous volume of information that is assembled. To better manage the data, and because better cameras are much more expensive, the resolution of satellite data is somewhat crude. (Of course, *crude* is a relative term, based on the purpose of your investigation.) Currently most satellite data is available at 10 meter or 30 meter resolution. Some of the best data will soon be available from new commercial satellites, and that data will have a resolution of one meter.

Remotely Sensed Data Are "Natural"

It is anticipated that remotely sensed data will continue to improve. There will be finer resolution of the data, and monitoring temporal change will become more codified. Access to data will improve, and the cost of data will decline. All of these advancements will benefit land planners, because natural data is currently more scarce than cultural data. Many cultural databases and their geo-referenced maps are already available for tax collection, the census, banking, crime statistics, 911 responses, health statistics, infrastructure management, and utilities distribution. Maps and databases of natural conditions exist, but at

Figure 11.1 Arkansas false color infrared GAP vegetation map.

very coarse resolution. What detailed GIS data does exist for natural themes is not universal, and the information is difficult to locate because the data have been generated on a project-by-project basis. It is anticipated that natural data will be more widely available, updated more frequently, and better adapted to the needs of the users (Mapping Science Committee 1997).

Another form of "remote sensing" is field monitoring. Instrumentation to monitor pollution, erosion, and natural systems will continue to emerge (ibid.). In April 1996 the Mapping Science Committee and the Federal Geographic Data Committee participated in a workshop to consider how the demands for data may change over the next 20 years. Here is a quote from their report:

> Environmental degradation and reduction in biological diversity will probably remain issues, with implications for the robustness of the environment and its ability to withstand change. To date, environmental concerns, monitoring, and mitigation efforts appear to be dominated by problems caused by point sources, such as smokestacks or effluent discharge pipes. The nonpoint-source problems of agricultural runoff, groundwater quality, and watershed management require very different approaches to monitoring and mitigation. Increased instrumentation and measurement of the environment will provide a more complete, higher-resolution picture of the world in which we live and one that is better suited to addressing nonpoint-source problems.

A GIS Crystal Ball

At that workshop four scenarios were examined, based on the work of Michael Wegner and Ian Masser (1996):

- The trend scenario—Essentially a continuation of existing trends, with data being widely available and GIS becoming more universal and transparent.
- The market scenario—Information would be controlled by wealthy corporations as a result of the public's demand for smaller government.
- The big brother scenario—Monitoring devices would record daily movements of vehicles and people in an effort to reduce crime and restore law and order.

- The beyond-GIS scenario—Data would be made available to service grass roots democracy in local-level decision making.

Implications?

What does this have to do with the way we do our work? Whether we use GIS or not, we are all dependent on data. CADD files are digital, and for most purposes they are now universal. The trend in GIS software is toward a seamless exchange of CADD and GIS data. Once the data has been enriched with GIS topology and attribute database formatting, it offers much greater complexity, many more quantifiable answers, and can be accurately interfaced with other data types. In many arenas, those professionals without GIS capability will be working at a distinct disadvantage.

Surfing for Fun and Profit

The Internet will continue to expand, and its services will proliferate. It is already possible to download data and public domain software from the Internet. It is anticipated that spatial analytical operators (see Chapter 6) will be available over the Internet, which will replace certain software products entirely. Research once done in a library is already done by surfing the net. Internet publications will require a new classification system. Findings and policies of organizations and individuals will be presented in cyberspace rather than at professional conferences, through blind peer review, or even under the editorial eye of major publishers. Standards have been developed for spatial data; they will have to be expanded to cover GIS supportive text and other cyberspace research materials as well.

File Transfer Protocol (FTP) already allows us to share data files over the net. The Internet permits us to pursue projects in more remote parts of the world, to work with experts on distant continents, and to attend meetings via interactive video. When better field monitoring devices are developed to assess natural conditions, the location from which we work will become less and less restrictive. Let us hope that site visits do not become passé or will not be considered too expensive.

Specific Site Design Advancements

What advances will directly affect the way site designers work? Several possibilities come to mind, although they all require major research and development efforts. It is the interaction between the computer people and the designers that is crucial to developing these and other innovations.

1. Existing databases can be used to generate land use standards based on local precedents.
2. Conversely, databases can be searched to identify existing inventories of uses, with an eye toward balance and/or diversity.
3. Advances in database structure, such as object-oriented databases, may lend themselves to planning models in more realistic ways than do relational databases.
4. Expert systems may be developed in ways that will automate the program analysis (the decision matrix and the ideal bubble diagram) in the design process. Once a body of work, including spatial decisions, has been generated in a GIS, decision support systems or neural networks may be employed to derive patterns from these decisions.
5. Because so many narrowly defined programs are becoming available, it is not unreasonable to think that the design process described in Chapter 10 will become a software application, leading the designer through the process and prompting him or her for decisions.

These possibilities are discussed further in the following paragraphs.

FINDING PATTERNS IN THE NUMBERS

When GIS data is available, it can be used in creative ways. Here is an example of using databases to develop standards that are unique to a town or rural area. This idea is based on a study done by the author to establish recreation standards in the town of Prairie Grove, Arkansas (Hanna 1993).

If a city has a GIS of all its publicly owned lands, it will have data on its parks and recreation facilities. If a new park is to be built, the number of certain facilities, such as tennis courts, may be determined by referring to published standards. Most states prepare a Statewide Comprehensive Outdoor Recreation Plan (SCORP) report on a five- or ten-year basis. However, the standards reflect an average for the state or region. The number of tennis courts required for a certain population size is generalized in this report.

A more appropriate indicator of the demand for tennis courts may be derived from the databases and use of local interviews. There are several indicators for tennis demand:

- Begin by locating existing public tennis facilities.
- Determine whether those facilities are well used or not, by interviewing operators and users.
- If well used, ascertain the demographics of the surrounding residents: age, income, education level, home ownership, etc.
- Determine the service area for each successful tennis club through interviews, and find the number of residents within that area by referring to census data.
- Compare the demographics of the area surrounding the selected site with those of the successful subject site.
- Use that information to develop a local standard for tennis demand.

As agencies are required to be ever more accountable to the public, this type of investigation becomes more essential in maintaining the goodwill of the citizens and in spending dwindling public dollars most effectively. GIS technology makes the exercise much quicker and easier to accomplish.

Recreation demand is changing rapidly. Twenty years ago there were hardly any soccer fields in local parks or on school grounds; now they're standard facilities. Other recent changes in recreation demand include mountain biking, skateboarding, and white-water sports. A cottage industry developing new standards would be very useful for park departments and recreation agencies, planning departments and the insurance industry.

WHEN IS ENOUGH ENOUGH?

The other side of the demand question is satisfaction through existing facilities. Again, a city's land use database will show how many facilities (tennis courts, softball fields, lit baseball fields, swimming pools, soccer fields, acres of picnic area, etc.) exist and where they are located in the city. The data will be available both in charts and on maps. Regardless of the method used to establish demand for each recreation type, the inventory of existing facilities can be compared with the demand.

You could take your study a step further and generate demographic profiles of each neighborhood and generate demand for each type of recreation within each neighborhood. The GIS could then be used to locate the nearest of each facility type. You could use a buffer analysis with a threshold distance to identify those facilities that are too far away to reasonably be used, especially by children. You would then have quantifiable data to support your citywide recreation master plan proposals.

OOPS!

Object-oriented programming (OOP) and object-oriented analysis (OOA) are being used to develop applications that emulate real-world conditions. Whereas relational databases are made up of tables with columns and rows, object-oriented databases are made up of individual data records that function more like targets. Each piece of data has the ability:

- To be abstracted: to ignore certain characteristics when it is advantageous to do so
- To be encapsulated: to protect the internal workings of the item
- To have inheritance: to allow the next generation of data to inherit characteristics of its parent
- To have association: to communicate with messages, scale, and behavior

The advantage of object oriented programming is that it automatically associates the right procedures with each object: c.draw uses the circle draw procedure because object c is a circle, but a.draw uses the point draw procedure because object a is a point (Covington and Downing 1992, 234).

Figure 11.2 *Outdoor Space and Facilities Matrix shows standards, deficiencies, and surpluses.*

ACTIVITIES	SPATIAL STANDARDS	CURRENT EXCESS (+) OR DEFICIT (–)	ACTIVITY ACREAGE	BUFFER ACREAGE	TOTAL ACREAGE
VERY LIGHT IMPACT					
1. Nature walks	50' wide 6.1 acres/mile - activity .6 acre/mile - buffer	–4.1 miles	–24.9 acres	–2.5 acres	–27.4 acres
2. Walking for pleasure	10' wide 1.2 acres/mile - activity .1 acre/mile - buffer	–81.09 miles	–97.5 acres	–8.5 acres	–106.0 acres
LIGHT IMPACT					
3. Informal recreation	.3 acre buffer/acre activity	+622.95 acres	+623.0 acres	+186.8 acres	+809.8 acres
4. Fishing from boats	1 acre water/2 boats 1 ramp/75 boats 1½ acres land/ramp	+ acres	+ acres	+ acres	+ acres
5. Hiking	10' wide 1.2 acres/mile - activity 2.3 acres/mile - buffer	–13.65 miles	–16.4 acres	–31.4 acres	–47.8 acres
6. Non-power boating	1 acre/2 boats 1 ramp/75 boats 1½ acres land/ramp	+ acres	+ acres	+ acres	+ acres
MODERATE IMPACT					
7. Power boating	1 acre/2 boats 1 ramp/75 boats 1½ acres land/ramp	+ acres	+ acres	+ acres	+ acres
8. Picnicking	10 tables/acre; 1 acre buffer/10 tables	–704 tables	–70.4 acres	–70.4 acres	–140.8 acres
9. Bicycling	10' wide 1.2 acres/mile - activity 2.3 acres/mile - buffer	–119.85 miles	–143.8 acres	–275.6 acres	–419.4 acres
10. Beach use	50' wide beach 6.1 acres/mile - activity 24.4 acres/mile - buffer	–1.93 sites	–11.8 acres	–47.1 acres	–58.9 acres
11. Horseback riding	10' wide 1.2 acres/mile - activity 2.3 acres/mile - buffer	–7.02 acres	–8.4 acres	–16.2 acres	–24.6 acres
TOTALS Light recreation - TOTAL ACRES			–373.2 acres	–451.7 acres	–824.9 acres
Light recreation - SUITABILITY GRID CELLS			65.0 grid cells	78.7 grid cells	143.7 grid cells
HEAVY IMPACT					
12. Group picnicking	10 tables/acre; 1 acre buffer/10 tables	–227 tables	–22.5 acres	–22.5 acres	–45 acres
13. Playing outdoor sports	3 acres buffer/acre activity	–80.28 acres	–80.3 acres	–240.8 acres	–321.1 acres
14. Swimming (in pools)	1 acre/pool 1 acre buffer/pool	–20 pools	–20 acres	–20 acres	–40 acres
15. Camping	10 sites/acre 1 acre buffer/10 sites	–1389 sites	–138.9 acres	–138.9 acres	–277.8 acres
16. Attending outdoor events	.5 acre buffer/acre activity	–1.8 acres	–1.8 acres	–.9 acres	–2.7 acres
17. OHV riding	10' wide trail 1 acre buffer/acre activity	–94 acres	–94 acres	–94 acres	–188 acres
TOTALS Heavy recreation - TOTAL ACRES			–357.5 acres	–517.1 acres	–874.6 acres
Heavy recreation - SUITABILITY GRID CELLS			62.3 grid cells	90.1 grid cells	152.4 grid cells

Designers need not become object-oriented programmers; they just need to work closely with one in order to explore this alternative database structure (Coad and Yourdon 1991). Object-oriented databases could be used to make more informed plant material selections and develop better specifications for maintenance and construction.

DEFER TO THE EXPERT

Expert systems are similar to object-oriented databases in that both emulate the multiple processes and outcomes possible in "the real world." Expert systems include (1) a user interface (menus, commands, or short-answer questions), (2) a knowledge base, and (3) an inference engine, which is used to draw conclusions "by performing simple logical operations on the knowledge base and the information supplied by the user" (Covington and Downing 1992). Expert systems are becoming widely used for everything from airline reservations to patient diagnosis.

Applying expert systems to analysis of a proposed program could be quite useful to site design. Decision matrices and bubble diagrams for very complex use programs could be generated through expert systems. The possibility exists for nonexperts to misrepresent the technology, but that is a consequence that the design professions will have to address through establishment of standards and ethics.

OFF-THE-SHELF SITE DESIGN

Commercial off-the-shelf (COTS) software has become extremely diversified. There are programs for very narrow segments of the market, as well as mammoth, comprehensive programs. The advantage of the programs for narrow segments is usually cost, and many have been quite successful. It is not unreasonable to think that a software package may appear that follows the step-by-step process described in detail in Chapter 10. If one did, I would have the same reservation as the engineer I recently spoke with in Memphis: "GIS has become so inexpensive that too many businesses are getting into it. Many inappropriate operators are producing GIS products, and they're telling the wrong story." His complaint seemed to be with locational studies done for retailers, whose work was not integrated in any way into citywide land use or traffic studies.

CHARLATANS AMONG US

The design process is not learned overnight. Most universities now require five years to complete an undergraduate degree in landscape architecture. All good site designers recognize that it takes another few years to learn the difference between the theories taught in school and the realities of practice. The decisions made at each step require experience, not just computer prompting. Site design is not multiple choice; it requires strict analysis based on research and experience; it requires visualization of the site and of the proposals for it; and it draws from historic and natural system precedents. Even if you were allowed to drive a formula one race car, you would not be safe behind the wheel without training and experience.

A computer program is no substitute for design ability. However, a good computer program can allow you to test many alternatives. It can give you hard answers in seconds, rather than hours. It can produce beautiful plans of alternative schemes with little effort and consistent quality. The right tool in the right hands can overcome barriers erected through poor communication and inadequate testing. "A fool with a tool is still a fool" (Coad and Yourdon 1991).

REFERENCES

Coad, Peter, and Edward Yourdon. 1991. *Object Oriented Design.* Englewood Cliffs, NJ: Yourdon Press,

Covington, Michael, and Douglas Downing. 1992. *Dictionary of Computer Terms,* 3d ed. Hauppauge, NY: Barron's.

Hanna, Karen C. 1993. "Using GIS and Relational Databases for Standards Development in Landscape Architecture." In *Proceedings of CELA 93.* Eugene, OR: Council of Educators in Landscape Architecture.

Mapping Science Committee. 1993. *Toward a Coordinated Spatial Data Infrastructure for the Nation.* Washington, DC: National Academy Press.

———. 1997. *The Future of Spatial Data and Society: Summary of a Workshop.* Washington, DC: National Academy Press.

Negroponte, Nicholas. 1995. *Being Digital.* New York: Vintage Books.

Thompson, J. William. 1996. "Reconsidering the Cutting Edge." *Landscape Architecture,* January.

Wegner, Michael, and Ian Masser. 1996. "Brave New GIS Worlds." In *GIS Diffusion: The Adoption and Use of Geographical Information Systems in Local Government in Europe,* ed. Ian Masser, Heather Campbell, and Max Craglia. London: Taylor & Francis.

Is GIS in Your Future?

At this time, the choice to use GIS as a tool for design is a personal one. Are you engaged in the type of work that lends itself to this technology? Is it the kind of work that interests you? Just what kind of work lends itself to GIS? Is it large-scale planning? Is it subdivision design or park design?

GIS technology supports work that needs justification of the choices made during the design process. It is work for which data and/or databases exist or can easily be created. It is work that demands the sophistication of professionals proficient in many areas: design, technical issues that support design, and the increasingly more accessible skills of the digital craft. Does this sound like all design work? Perhaps it is!

Not every firm will benefit from GIS. Some are not in a position to recoup the cost of hardware, software, and training. The nature of some practices does not require statistical reporting or complex mapping. Custom residential design firms probably would not benefit from GIS, but they certainly could use three-dimensional CADD capabilities, and GIS viewshed analysis could be useful on occasion.

It is difficult to remember when CADD programs did not have 3-D capabilities, and now that feature is taken for granted. Several software developers are merging CADD and GIS in common, interchangeable programs. Few GIS packages these days are just raster or just vector; most have components of each. The labels "CADD," "GIS," "terrain analysis," and "3-D modeling" are becoming part of the comprehensive term "spatial analysis." GIS may be less imposing when it is part of a multi-faceted software package with capabilities for spatial analysis, data synthesis, graphic display, map production, mensuration, and reporting. All software is moving toward universal access rather than segmentation.

Whether or not one should commit to GIS is becoming a small question. The big question is, "Can I work that way? Can I use digital information and computer operations to do what I've always done in my head and with a pencil in my hand? Do I want to work that way?" I suspect your first response is "No!" You are certainly not alone in your reluctance to try a Geographic Information System.

The process that is documented in Chapter 10 was developed specifically to allow designers to work more comfortably in GIS. It was developed by an experienced site designer. The process has been utilized and has been well received by clients and citizens.

GIS data is becoming much more available. The means to effect GIS (hardware, software, training) are becoming more accessible. Some clients already demand GIS; others currently make it optional. The greatest danger to design professionals is that other disciplines will do their work and will do it poorly. Those who have GIS will be able to respond to certain RFPs (requests for proposals) and those without will not. The non-GIS'ers may lose more than a single project; they may lose the ongoing ability to do that type of work and perhaps the ability to work for that client.

How will GIS reshape the worlds of landscape architecture, planning, engineering, and architecture? Will it cause a schism between the digital and the nondigital? CADD has not done that. Will it make designers more proficient? Not by itself. But the potential is there to make the work much more accountable. With greater access to more facts, our decision making can become more objective. With greater interaction with other GIS-ing disciplines, we can integrate our efforts into more comprehensive design and management projects.

Perhaps the nature of development will evolve toward a more comprehensive view of the spatial realm. Rather than being driven by individual owners and enterprises, the reality of integrating natural, social, biotic, and economic systems will come to fruition. Is GIS a revolution? It can be if we look at it as a tool for unification of the design professions. GIS has to be explored by creative people, those who will take its evolution toward a synthesis of the physical and cultural worlds in which we live.

ACCESS

1. Ability of a computer to reference a specific data set (single record, file, group of files, other) by identifying a specific sector of memory or the disk drive (server) where it is stored for the purpose of editing, assembling, manipulating, and/or directing this data set to a peripheral devise.

2. Portion of the operating system dedicated to locating a body of data and making it available to the user for viewing, analyzing, and/or editing purposes.

ACCURACY Closeness of results of observations, computations, or estimation of spatial features to their true value of position. "Absolute accuracy" is the differential between the actual real world location of a point on the surface of the earth and its mathematically assigned geographic coordinate.

ADDRESS MATCHING Process that compares a table of addresses to the address attributes of a theme to convert textual addresses to locations on a map. Street name and address values are compared with DBMS records to find the street segment with a matching name and address range. The address is then located at a prorated distance from the street segment's startpoint proportional to the address's value relative to the street's address range value and on the appropriate side of the street (even addresses always on the right, etc.)

* Provided by Dennis Klein, Urban and Regional Information Systems Association 1460 Renaissance Drive, Suite 305 Park Ridge, Illinois 60068, or (www.urisa.org)

ALGORITHM Step-by-step problem-solving procedure, especially an established, recursive computational procedure for solving a problem. Set of ordered procedures, steps, or rules, usually applied to mathematical calculations, assumed to lead to the solution of a problem in a finite number of steps; the logic (and/or formula) that is used to solve a problem. Typical algorithms possess the following characteristics:

- Application to a particular problem results in a finite sequence of steps.
- Unique initial step. Predicated on the results it derives, each step has a unique successor.
- Terminates with either the solution or an error message stating that the problem has no solution.

ALPHANUMERIC Combination of alphabetic letters, numbers, and/or special characters. A mailing address is an alphanumeric listing. The designation ljsdoijwe92393 is an alphanumeric word. Alphabetic characters consist of letters A through Z; numeric characters consist of the characters 0 through 9. Alphanumeric systems sometimes exclude () and *∧.

AM/FM Acronym for Automated Mapping/Facility Management, a computer-based Land Information System (LIS). It is used to produce, edit, archive, and correlate automated map features with nongraphic-facility-related design or operation attributes. Primarily applies to systems that support infrastructure operations. Spatial data management system that supports the utility and public works operations, maintenance, planning, analysis, and accountability of utility infrastructure systems such as sewer, water, natural gas, telephone and cable networks, electrical, and storm drainage.

ANALOG In the context of remote sensing and GIS, refers to data in graphical or pictorial form, as opposed to digital form. Generally, refers to a quantity that is continuously variable, rather than one that varies only in discrete steps.

ANNOTATION Text or labels plotted graphically on a map or drawing. Text labels for naming such map features as streets and places; unique identification numbers assigned to individual map features including parcels, utility nodes, and links; dimensioning; posted notes and instructions; descriptive text used to label area features such as soil types, zoning categories. Annotations are typically map features that are not linked to DBMS records.

APPLICATION Use of software, data, procedures, and techniques in a series of steps that are then put into practice to solve a problem or perform a function.

1. Of or being a computer program designed for a specific task or use.

APPLICATION SOLUTION A combination of spatial data structures, symbol libraries, data dictionaries, attribute formats, linked DBMS configurations, menus, icons, dialogs, software executables, productivity enhancements, tutorials, and focused documentation that together provide a total environment for building, maintaining, and operating a GIS or AM/FM database.

ARC Locus of points that forms a linear feature in a spatial database that is not closed.

1. A set of XY coordinates used to represent a linear feature or a polygon boundary. It is a continuous string of XY coordinate pairs (vertices) beginning at one location and ending at another location, having length but no area.

2. A coverage feature class used to represent linear features and polygon boundaries. One linear feature can contain many arcs.

3. In CAD it is a curvalinear feature defined by such location combinations as center point, radius, and starting point.

ARCHITECTURE Set of data, processes, and technologies that together make up the physical and communication system supporting information management operations. There are data architectures for the database system. There are software architectures that support the computation, analysis, and processing aspects of the organization. There are technology architectures that support the hardware and network configurations.

ASCII Acronym for the "American Standard Code for Information Interchange," a standard way to represent text. Because ASCII text contains no formatting (fonts, underlines, or special characters), it can be read by all computers. A convention for using digital data to represent printable characters that provide compatibility for data communications. Used for information interchange between different computer systems. A set of 128 characters used for communication between computers and word processing systems. An ASCII File, also referred to as a text file, is made up of text records each of which contains only letters, numbers, punctuation symbols, and control codes.

ASPECT

1. Horizontal direction in which a slope faces; or the exposure, commonly expressed in degrees clockwise from North.
2. Compass direction facing downward in the direction of the steepest slope (maximum rate of decent. For example, if the declination from North of the steepest gradient were 90 degrees, the aspect (or exposure) would be West facing. Aspect maps display the general orientation of each area of land typically according to eight regimes: N, NW, W, SW, S, SE, E, NE.

ATTRIBUTE(S)

1. Single element of nongraphic data assigned to a spatial feature either as an imbedded data element within the spatial database or located in a linked DBMS data record.
2. Descriptive characteristics of a feature, site, or phenomenon. Location is a mandatory attribute.
3. Set or collection of data that describe the characteristics of real-world conditions.

BASE MAP

1. Basic representation of a region of the earth as it would appear if viewed from above.
2. Portrays basic reference information onto which other information of a specialized nature is placed. Usually shows the location and extent of natural earth surface features and permanent man-made objects.
3. Contains basic digital survey control and topographic elevation reference framework for integrating all of the other map features of a particular geographic area.

BLOCK GROUP U.S. Census Bureau term that refers to a set of U.S. census blocks combined to provide a small population and housing census area. All selected census blocks are contained within a single census tract boundary containing an average of population of 800(+/−), about one fourth to one fifth the population of a census tract.

BOOLEAN OPERATIONS

1. Of or relating to a logical combinatorial system that treats variables such as propositions and computer logic elements, through the operators AND, OR, NOT, IF, THEN, and EXCEPT.

2. Within multiple sets of polygon features, operations that produce their union, intersection, complement, and exclusion.

BUFFER

1. Area within a specified distance (radius) around a selected map feature or features.

2. Operation that creates a new entity by tracing around an entity or entities at a constant distance. For example, the buffer around a point is a circle.

CAD Acronym for Computer Aided Drafting, a computer-aided process for interactively creating, modifying, and manipulating spatial information. Mathematical integrity of the spatial model is adequate to support legal survey and engineering design requirements.

CAD/GIS Refers to integrating Geographic Information System technology with that of Computer Aided Design Systems.

CADASTRE Official map record pertaining to location, quantity, value, and ownership of land parcels within a government jurisdiction. Polygon overlay of parcel boundaries, each containing a PIN (Parcel ID Number), linked nongraphic DBMS tables of supporting land tenure, and other pertinent information for the primary purpose of taxation. *See* Multipurpose Cadastre.

CALIBRATION

1. In vector mapping, the adjustment of the digitizing tablet so that a location on the manual map corresponds to the location of the cursor within the display of the spatial database. To implement, XY values of known coordinates within the survey control network are entered in conjunction with screen selections of the corresponding locations on the map sheet to be digitized.

2. In remote sensing, these are parameters pertaining to spectral and/or geometric characteristics of a sensor or radiation source.

CAMA Accronym for Computer Aided Mass Appraisal, a standard for managing Assessors' information. The CAMA Interface Direct Query Application (CIDQA) is used to analyze CAMA data.

CARTESIAN COORDINATE Point whose location is expressed in terms of its distance above or below an X, a Y, and/or a Z coordinate plane. Location of a point on a plane is expressed by two coordinate values, one representing the distance from the Y axis and the other representing the distance from the X axis.

CARTOGRAPHY Science and art of making maps and charts. More broadly, the term includes all the steps necessary to produce a map: planning, aerial photography, drafting, editing, color separation, and multicolored printing. In regard to computerized spatial databases, a cartospatial feature is a point, line, arc, string, chain, polygon, symbol, text, or other form of spatial entity. Functionality of cartographic information systems is limited to encoding, displaying, and measuring cartospatial features.

CELL

1. Basic element of spatial information in a grid data set. A cell map is generally made up of a spatial grid of rectilinear spatial units (sometimes square) of the same size and shape, each depicting a condition assigned to all areas within the cell relative to a selected measurement. Such values are typically stored in a linked attribute table.
2. The location of a single value in a database defined by intersecting a row or record with a field or column.

CENSUS DATA Official, usually periodic, enumeration of a population, often including the collection of related demographic information. The U.S. Census Bureau conducts a census of the U.S. population every 10 years and publishes detailed descriptions of subgroups within the overall population for a variety of purposes. The Census Bureau organizes this data according to the following hierarchy of designated census areas:

Census Tract: Subarea of a county or city containing an average of approximately 4,000 inhabitants who have statistically comparable population characteristics, economic status, and living conditions.

Block Group: Subset of a Census Tract containing a population of approximately 800.

Census Block: Subset of a Block Group, the smallest geographic area for which census data is collected.

CENTERLINE Linear feature representing the midpoint along a linear element like a road or stream.

CENTROID Any point used to label the location of a feature in a spatial database (polygon, line, or point). The geometric center of a polygon; may be calculated as the average location of all vertices of a polygon boundary. Any single location within a polygon, arithmetically derived or not, to which attribute information about that polygon area is linked. Midpoint of a line to which attribute information about that line is linked.

CHARACTER STRING A consecutive sequence of alphanumeric characters (i.e., ABC, def, 123) used together as a single unit for purposes of display or analysis.

CLEAN Refers to data that are devoid of errors. Process for identifying and correcting potential errors in digital map line work. For example, closed polygon areas made up of boundary segments wherein the location of the end point of one segment is identical with the start point of the next segment. In other words, line work free of gaps and dangles.

CLIENT/SERVER

1. Refers to communications between computers. The client computer is typically a desktop microcomputer device using a software program to contact and obtain data from a server computer. The server is typically a minicomputer, workstation, or mainframe computer integrated over a network. However, the server can be a microcomputer linked to multiple storage devices.

2. In context with the Internet, the client is any computer that can access an Internet service. For example, there are Gopher clients and Telnet clients. The server is a central computer from which a particular service origi-

nates. For example, there are FTP servers and Gopher servers.

COGO   Acronym for Coordinate Geometry. COGO is a subsystem of CAD or GIS made up of a set of standard procedures for processing survey data such as bearings, distances, and angles to generate precise spatial representation of land features and survey control networks.

COMPOSITE MAPPING   Overlaying and combining data types from two or more map overlays to create a map displaying:

1. Combination of each map's characteristics.
2. Combination of information from different thematic maps.
3. The combined characteristics of multiple overlapping spatial data layers.

COMPUTER AIDED DRAFTING (CAD)   Computer-aided process for creating, modifying, and manipulating spatial information. Typical operations are interactive, whereby a user either requests immediate results in the creation of new spatial features or modification of existing spatial features. The mathematical integrity of the spatial model is adequate to support legal survey and engineering design requirements.

CONFLATE (OR CONFLATION)   To meld or fuse two or more components into one whole. In regard to GIS, to merge two or more spatial data sets into one.

CONFORMAL PROJECTION   A projection wherein the scale is the same in every direction at any point. Meridians and parallels intersect at right angles; the shape of small areas and angles with very short sides are preserved. Most area values are distorted.

CONIC PROJECTION   A projection in which the surface is drawn as it would appear if projected on a cone wrapped around the earth. A Lambert projection is a form of conic projection often used for maps of the continental United States, France, and other countries.

CONNECTIVITY   Topological property of lines and nodes being linked or attached to each other, typically pertaining to infrastructure networks such as utility and transportation systems.

CONTINUOUS MAP   Treats an entire service territory as one large map and, hence, one large file. More complex than tiled mapping systems because of the need to reference the entire database in order to act on any one part of it.

CONTOUR MAPPING   Display of contour lines, each of which represents a constant value, typically elevation, throughout its length. Also called an Isoline map, it displays linear features that connect all points having the same numeric value (i.e., elevation, rainfall, noise, concentration level).

CONVERSION   Translating manually displayed spatial information (handdrawn maps and diagrams) into digital spatial databases.

CORRIDOR ANALYSIS   Procedure used to identify the extents of corridors of land area containing candidate routes for such linear transportation features as highways, pipelines, and electric transmission. Land use/environmental data overlays are prepared for the areas within the selected corridors, which are subsequently used to determine explicit and relative measurements for comparing alternative routes and assessing the selected route in terms of construction cost, environmental impact, and operational effectiveness.

COVERAGE   A spatial data set of similar geographic features and/or variables represented within a GIS. Includes mapped graphics linked to an attribute database.

CYLINDRICAL PROJECTION   A mathematical projection of the earth onto a cylinder, tangent at the equator. Often used to represent the entire earth in a rectangular frame, and is very popular for world maps.

DATA   General term for information, including facts, measurements, classifications, and value representations, from which conclusions can be inferred. Things known about real-world entities; results of observations or measurements of such features. A single datum has three potential components:

1. *Attributes,* attributes describing the substance characteristics, variables, values, and similar qualities of the datum.
2. *Geographic,* information describing the position of the datum in space relative to other data.

3. *Temporal,* information describing the instant or period of time for which the datum is valid.

DATABASE DESIGN   Structure of a database. In spatial data management systems, refers to both the spatial and tabular parts. A collection of interrelated data sets stored together and controlled by a specific schema for efficient management of information. A consistent and specified set of procedures is used in building, maintaining, accessing, and interrogating information from a database.

DATABASE MANAGEMENT SYSTEM (DBMS)   A computer-based system or application software that enables users to build and maintain a nonspatial database. The DBMS performs a variety of data access, edit, query, and reporting operations. DBMS can also refer to the collection of software required to use and manipulate tabular databases to present multiple different views of the data.

DATUM

1. Point, line, or surface used as a reference for a measurement of another quantity. Point, line, or surface used as a reference (i.e., surveying, mapping, or geology).
2. Combination of parameters and control points used to accurately define the three-dimensional shape of the earth (spheroid). For example, the North American Datum for 1983 (NAD83) is the basis for map projections and coordinates within the United States and throughout North America.

DBMS RECORD   In the context of spatial databases, a record in a data table external to the spatial database that contains attribute information corresponding to a specific map feature.

DECISION SUPPORT SYSTEM   Focuses on complex decision-making situations and the problems most often faced by an organization's decision makers. A computerized process designed to provide decision makers with what they need to know when they need to know it, including pertinent, up-to-date maps, tables, graphs, photos, histograms, and charts to make the most informed decision possible. An automatically designated value, setting, or an action automatically taken, unless otherwise specified. Values or parameter settings defined by the software vendor or the system user that are applied automatically during data entry, editing, and/or analysis operations unless changed by the user. For example, a default snap radius is set at 5 model units unless the current polygon processing transaction requires a different one to be applied. For data models there can be default symbol libraries, file and attribute naming conventions, DBMS configurations, interface links, and spatial database formatting schemes.

DEMOGRAPHIC Data characteristics of human populations, such as size, growth, density, distribution, and vital statistics. Sociologic/economic data concerning the human environment.

DENSITY MAP Symbols produced randomly in polygons or grid cells with each symbol representing a numerical count (i.e., ten households, one gas station).

DIGITAL DATA Anything in computer readable format, usually stored on magnetic tape or disk. Spatial or attribute data stored in electronic format, digital units, on a hard drive. Discrete numerical representation of information versus analog representation.

DIGITAL ELEVATION MODEL (DEM) Digital cartographic representation of a terrain surface or a subsurface feature as defined by a series of three-dimensional coordinate values. A digital representation of a continuous variable over a two-dimensional surface by a regular array of Z values referenced to a common datum.

DIGITIZE Process of tracing hard copy documents on a tablet to capture line work in digital form. The process of converting existing data from paper maps, aerial photos, or raster images into digital form by tracing the maps on a digitizer. Feature locations are encoded as X, Y coordinates.

DIME FILE DIME is an acronym for Dual Independent Map Encoding, a data format used by the U.S. Census Bureau to encode street network and related data for the 1980 Census. *See* TIGER for details.

DISSOLVE To remove boundaries between adjacent polygons having the same value for a specific attribute. To combine polygons that would otherwise be assigned the same color or hatch pattern in a thematic map display. Process of aggregating neighboring polygons based on a matching value for some attribute.

DRAPING   Display of selected two-dimensional data on a perspective view of certain relief or any other spatially distributed variable. For example, a map of a road network may be draped over a perspective view of a 3-D terrain surface.

DRAWING FILE   Digital CAD equivalent of a hard copy document. Some systems refer to drawing files as designs or design files. A collection of graphical features stored as a set of spatial information in a computer.

DTM   Acronym for Digital Terrain Model, a representation of terrain relief in a computer readable format. Also referred to as a Digital Elevation Model.

DXF   Acronym for Data Exchange Format, a standard spatial data exchange format for CAD systems. DXF files contain ASCII or binary (DXB) records, each of which describes a vector complete enough that it can be converted into a spatial feature by any spatial database management product able to process these files.

DYNAMIC SEGMENTATION   Functionality for modeling linear features in a transportation or other network-related applications. Process of dynamically locating events along linear features straight from attribute tables in which attributes are recorded according to distance from a start point. The ability to translate data collection in linear (milepost) measures into:

- Posted point and symbol features adjacent to an alignment representing incidents or facilities
- Break points along an alignment wherein each resulting route segment has a unique set of assigned physical and/or operational attributes

EASTING/NORTHING   Within a State Plane coordinate system, the easting and northing coordinates of a location are describing the distance from an origin point.

EDGE MATCHING   Map cleanup function that allows for distortion between adjacent maps to produce a true match of features at the edges of maps. The result is a continuous map, by ensuring that all features that cross the boundary between two adjacent maps appear to be or are a single feature.

FORMAT The physical structure of an item. The order in which information is prepared and presented.

1. The arrangement of data for storage or display. A file format is the specific design of how information is organized in a collection or set of related digital data.
2. To divide (a disk) into marked sectors so that it may store data.
3. To determine the arrangement of data for storage or display.

FRACTAL A geometric pattern that is repeated at ever smaller scales to produce irregular shapes and surfaces that cannot be represented by classical geometry. Fractals are used especially in computer modeling of irregular patterns and structures in nature.

FTP Acronym for File Transfer Protocol, a standardized way of transmitting files on the Internet.

GENERALIZATION Wherein a general class contains constituent classes.

1. In thematic mapping, boundaries between polygons that contain like attributes are dissolved (i.e., all categories of residential land are generalized under the simpler classification of residential; all categories of sanitary sewers are mapped as a single utility type.
2. The process of simplifying line work by removing or combining vertices. This can be done manually or automatically.

GEOCODING In spatial databases, a coding process wherein a digital map feature is assigned an attribute to serve as a unique ID (tract number, node number) or classification (soil type, zoning category). In polygon processing, the polygon boundary that contains the coordinate pair of a data item (text label) is assigned the value of that data item as "geocode."

GEODESY Science or art of measuring the shape and size of the earth's surface, or large parts of it, as distinguished from surveying, which deals only with limited tracts of the earth.

GEOGRAPHIC DATA MODEL Geographic Data Model (GDM) total combination of spatial data structures, symbol libraries, data dictionaries, attribute formats, linked SQL DBMS configurations, menus, icons, dialogs, software executables, and productivity enhancements that together provide an overall framework for building, maintaining, and operating an AM/FM or GIS database.

GEOGRAPHIC INFORMATION SYSTEM (GIS) *Note:* The following is not an attempt to provide a single generic definition.

1. Computerized decision support systems that integrate spatially referenced data. These systems capture, store, retrieve, analyze, and display spatial data.

2. An organized assemblage of computer hardware, software, spatial data, and operating instructions designed for capturing, storing, updating, manipulating, analyzing, and displaying all forms of geographically referenced information.

3. A manual or computer-based system for geographic data input, storage, manipulation, analysis, modeling, and output. The system is used to improve geographic question asking and problem solving and to enhance the overall geographic decision-making process.

GNIS Acronym for Geographic Name Information System.

GRID CELL MAP A map displaying spatial information in the form of color-coded, equal-sized rectangles, squares, equilateral triangles, or hexagons. The color of the cell is determined by the condition assigned to the cell according to a uniformly applied rule regarding the condition (i.e., geologic classification):

■ Present in the center of the cell, or

■ Makes up the greatest percentage of the cell area as compared with the other conditions present, or

■ Determined by a scoring system applied to selected spatial overlays. *See* Relative Suitability.

HIERARCHICAL DATABASE

1. A branching information storage system such that one record serves as the base. From this parent record, the data structure branches out to reference subordinate child records, which in turn branch out to more detailed records.

2. Database system in which the most significant information is stored in the most easily accessible location and the less significant, dependent data is stored in subordinate, less accessible locations.

INFORMATION Collection of data organized in a manner that is used to support the decision-making process. Knowledge derived from experience, instruction, and or study. Communication of knowledge. Data processed into a more meaningful form through comparison, summary, classification, and association.

INFORMATION SYSTEM Computer system that has the ability to perform data collection, assembly, interrogation, visualization, and communication.

INTERNET Worldwide international communications network comprised of thousands of government, academic, and private networks, each of which is using TCP/IP protocols. *See* TCP/IP.

INTEROPERABILITY Communication between different computer systems. Seamless accessing and sharing of multiple data structures across multiple hardware platforms, operating systems, and application software. For example, software A using hardware B being able to access and operate on data C.

INTERPOLATION Process of inserting, estimating, or finding a value intermediate to the values of two or more known points in space. Estimation of an elevation value at an unsampled point based on the known elevation values of surrounding points. Process of inserting, estimating, or finding a value intermediate to the values of two or more known points in space.

INTERSECTION Set of elements that contains elements shared by two or more given sets of elements. In spatial analysis, polygons within two or more overlays are combined to form a composite polygon overlay made up of an array of closed "sub-area" polygons, each of which is assigned a list of attributes that describe the combination of conditions present within its boundary. Such attribute tables may reside in external DBMS or tables stored within the spatial database.

INTRANET Any two or more computer networks connected together.

LAND COVER Environmental data overlay that defines the surface of the earth in terms of vegetation type in nondeveloped areas (i.e., forest, rowcrops, orchards, grasslands) and land use type in developed areas (residential, transportation, vacant, light industrial). Land cover map overlays can be derived from interpretation and classification of remotely sensed images.

LINE In spatial databases, a linear vector with only a start and an end point, containing no intermediary (shape) turning points. A line feature is the alignment between two points representing within a spatial database a real-world or theoretical feature; e.g., a road, stream, or parcel boundary.

LINE SMOOTHING A variety of smoothing algorithms used to reduce file size by removing excessive turning points along a linear feature according to a user-defined filter algorithm.

LIS Acronym for Land Information System. Manual or computer-based information system used to store, retrieve, display, and plot spatial and textural data relating primarily to land features and characteristics. Addresses a wide range of existing natural and cultural aspects of land within a mapped area, including property ownership, tax assessment, zoning, land use, vegetation, soils, geology, hazardous areas, noise zones, surface and subsurface hydrology, flora and fauna, visually and/or ecologically sensitive areas. Can also include overlays that address infrastructure systems, including transportation, sewer, water, storm, electric, cable, telephone, and storm drainage.

LOCATION
1. Distinct place in the real world
2. Position defined by a set of coordinates within a spatial database (i.e., pole, property corner, reported crime incident)
3. The storage space of digital data within an information storage system

LOGICAL CONNECTION Within a utility network topology, if the position setting of a link physically connected to a node is defined as "On" relative to that node, then this link is logically connected to that node.

MACROS
1. Sequence of commands executed as one command
2. Series of specialized procedures or instructions in a computer language that can be replaced by a set of

instructions that customize and streamline basic software functions

3. Recorded, often complex, sequence of keystrokes and mouse actions that can be played back with a single or simple combination of keystrokes.

MAINFRAME   Central Processing Unit, main memory, and control units of a computer, typically housed in one large cabinet or in a number of smaller ones grouped together. The term applies only to large computers.

MAP   Representation, usually on a plane surface, of a region of the earth or the heavens. Within a spatial database, an assembly of digital spatial features that represent a set of real-world features and the geographic relationships between them. This representation may exit digitally, manually (i.e., on paper), or in the human mind.

MAPEMATICS   Mathematics used in conjunction with creating maps, measuring map features, defining map accuracy, or other mapping functions that require quantification.

MARK   Character or feature in a file or record used to locate a specific point or condition.

MATRIX
1. Rectangular array of numeric or algebraic quantities subject to mathematical operations
2. Something resembling such an array, as in the regular formation of elements into columns and rows
3. Network of intersections between input and output leads in a computer, functioning as an encoder or a decoder

META-DATA   Data about data. This often includes the data's source, accuracy, data type, projection, date of origination, and other general descriptions.

MICROCOMPUTER   Very small computer, such as a laptop or personal computer, built around a microprocessor as its CPU and designed to be used by one person at a time; smaller than a minicomputer.

MINICOMPUTER   A medium-sized computer, usually fitting within a single cabinet, serving the needs of multiple users within a small organizational unit. Has more memory and a higher execution speed than a microcomputer. Also referred to as a workstation or midrange.

MIPS Acronym for Millions of Instructions per Second, a CPU-related performance measurement.

MODELING

1. Applying structured rules and procedures to one or more spatial database overlays to conduct spatial and/or network analysis to derive new information to aid in problem solving and planning.
2. Schematic description of a system, theory, or phenomenon that accounts for its known or inferred properties and may be used for further study of its operational characteristics.
3. Process of simulation, prediction, and description involving changing the parameters and generating/communicating new model results. Using spatial or network overlays to simulate a process to predict outcomes to what-if scenarios.

MODEM Abbreviation for MODulator and DEModulator, a device that converts data from one form into another.

1. From one form usable in data processing to another form usable in telephonic transmission
2. Send and receive information over communication lines between computers, usually over telephone lines

MOSAIC Public Domain World Wide Web browser with graphic capabilities (gif but not jpeg) developed by the National Center for Supercomputing Applications (NCSA) at the University of Illinois at Urbana—Champaign and available for general use at no charge.

MULTIMEDIA SYSTEM Combined use of several media types, such as video, computer graphics, animation, movies, slides, music, and lighting, especially for the purpose of education or entertainment. Integrating multiple technologies on a single platform with a single user interface.

MULTIPURPOSE CADASTRE Comprehensive land information system at the parcel level. Land base includes all parcel boundaries, rights-of-way, and easements with each parcel typically linked to supporting attribute records. Other components typically include highly precise survey control network and other information overlays addressing a wide range of natural and cultural characteristics, as well as supporting infrastructure systems.

NETWORK ANALYSIS   Specialized queries that reference connected linear and node features.

1. Typical analytical transactions within transportation networks:

   Modifying direction and/or impedance along links and through intersections.

   Identifying the optimal path as measured between two or more points according to a selected terms of measurement. Highlighting all components (nodes and links) of the optimal path, referred to as "routing."

2. Typical analytical transactions within utility networks:

   Modifying direction and ON/OFF position settings of links relative to nodes.

   Isolating all network nodes and links both physically and logically connected to a selected test point. Highlighting all logically connected network features, referred to as "network tracing." Attribute records linked to highlighted features can be subsequently isolated to perform design analysis.

3. Two types of utility networks:

   Pressure Networks. Typical transactions include resetting valves to redirect service operations or reset switches to reconfigure circuits. Typically applies to water, gas, steam, electric, and telephone systems.

   Gravity Networks. Typical transactions include isolating all nodes and links upstream or downstream from a test point. Can include isolating a portion of the network by changing position settings of links relative to their upstream or downstream nodes to OFF. Typically applies to sewer, storm, telephone, and, sometimes, electric utilities.

4. Typical analysis performed using records linked to highlighted features in a route or trace include load loss, traffic demand and capacity, pressure loss, maximum flow, gradient, asset management, and other engineering analysis.

PROJECTION   Mathematical method for representing the shape of the earth on a flat plane; a formula that converts latitude-longitude locations on the earth's spherical surface to X,Y locations on a map's flat surface. A system of intersecting lines, such as the grid of a map, on which part or all of the globe or another spherical surface is represented as a plane surface. The result may have distortion in distance, area, orientation, and/or scale. *See* Conformal, Conic, and Cylindrical Projections.

RASTER

1. Images containing individual dots with color values, called cells (or pixels), arranged in a rectangular, evenly spaced array. Aerial photographs and satellite images are examples of raster images used in mapping.

2. Method for storing spatial data that involves assigning a value to each dot in a large matrix. This method is very useful for modeling continuous phenomena like elevation of temperature.

RECORD

1. An assemblage of textual data within a DBMS table and/or drawn statement as a means of preserving knowledge.

2. Collected and preserved data describing a particular subject.

3. A row (series of field values) in a database table. In a spatial database, each graphic feature may be linked to one or more records in one or more tables.

4. A collection of fields or other subportion of computer file treated as a data unit.

RECTIFICATION   A set of techniques for removing data errors though calculation or adjustment. In image processing, computer programs that remove distortion within a digital image, aerial photography, or remotely sensed data by removing parallax errors due to relief (high ground being closer to the camera than low-lying areas), camera tilt, corner, and other distortions.

RELATIONAL DATABASE   Information storage system in which there is an association between two or more things. Organized according to relationships between data items. Collection of tables that are logically associated to each other by common attributes. By entering the table name, attribute name, and the value of the primary key, any data element or set of elements can be retrieved. Consists of table rows and columns.

RELATIVE SUITABILITY   A DBMS query based on a scoring system that generates a relative suitability (multivariable thematic) map. The technique involves:

- Assigning raw scores to values within a DBMS field. For example, rating a soil type as having a value of 4 on a scale of 10 regarding its development suitability; making the raw score of a parcel's land value equal to its land value.
- Assigning relative importance values to a DBMS field.
- Using values in each record to calculate a composite weighted raw score for each field involved.
- Determining the number and limits of regime ranges.
- Determining display parameters for suitability map (i.e., different colored pipes, roadway segments, parcel, or intersected polygons as colored lines, solid fills, and/or hatch patterns).

REMOTE SENSING   Using a recording device not in physical contact with the surface being analyzed, including:

1. Using sensors sensitive to various bands of the electro-magnetic spectrum
2. Assessing its spectral image without having the sensor in direct contact with the surface.
3. Interpreting environmental conditions at, below, and above the surface of the earth, typically by processing images from an aircraft (i.e., aerial photography), satellite imaging, or radar.

RESOLUTION   Fineness of detail that can be distinguished in an image, as on a video display terminal.

1. *Display Resolution.* The density of the pixels that compose an image. The greater the number of pixels per square inch of screen, the greater the resolution. In print, resolution is measured in dots per inch (dpi).
2. *Spatial Resolution.* The smallest possible map feature that can be accurately displayed at a specified map scale. For example, in a 1:24000 scale map, a 50-foot distance between a roadway and a railroad track centerline is one fortieth of an inch. Since the thinnest pen line width is presumed to be one fortieth of an inch, it is impossible to accurately represent the alignment of these two cen-

terlines and still have a visible gap between them. To do this takes a smaller map scale (<1:24000).

RUBBER SHEETING   Spatial database editing software that attempts to correct errors by stretching a map to fit known control points or monuments. Mathematical method to stretch or warp images to match existing vector data. Forces a digital map to fit a designated base. To implement, XY values of known coordinates within the survey control network are entered in conjunction with screen selections of the corresponding locations within the map overlay to be rubber sheeted. Each coordinate within the map overlay being processed is moved to the location of the prescribed control coordinate. A deformation (typically least square) algorithm is applied to translate, rotate, and/or rescale all other map features in a manner intended to minimize distortion.

SCALE

1. Relationship between the dimensions of a feature on a map and the geographic features they represent on the earth, commonly expressed as a fraction. For example, a map scale of 1:24000 means that one unit of measure on the map equals 24000 of the same unit on the earth (1 inch would equal 24000 inches = 2000 feet).

2. A calibrated line, as on a map or an architectural plan, indicating such a proportion.

3. Description of how length in the real world is related to length on a map. This can be portrayed in a variety of ways, including a representational fraction.

SENSITIVITY ANALYSIS   Multiple scoring systems (*see* Relative Suitability) are applied to a data model to generate multiple relative suitability maps, the scoring system for each being based on such "agendas" as:

- Developers wanting minimum cost and maximum amenity
- Local community wanting minimum neighborhood impacts
- Environmental lobbies wanting minimum regional impacts
- Local governments wanting maximum tax revenues and minimum service obligations/liabilities

Maps displaying best to worse relative suitability for each scoring system are generated and compared. With enough polygons, some will be allocated to the lowest or highest regime on all of them. Isolation of such areas serves as a starting point for building broad constituency for best-use recommendations.

SLOPE ANALYSIS   Type of terrain analysis in which the change in elevation of the ground over distance is determined. Measured in terms of a ratio of rise or fall within a horizontal distance (run), expressed as decimal, fraction, percentage, or the tangent of the angle of inclination. A slope map is depicted as a polygon overlay, with each polygon geocoded according to the range of slope of the ground within its boundary. (i.e., 0–10%, 10–20%, etc.).

SMART CAD   CAD system that has the capability to link spatial elements with relational databases.

SPATIAL ANALYSIS

1. Methods used to explore the spatial relationships between features both real and theoretical
2. Process of extracting or creating new information about a set of geographic features; techniques to determine the distribution of a spatial feature(s); and the relationships between two or more features, the location of, proximity to, and orientation of these features in space
3. Study of the locations and shapes of geographic features and the relationships between them

SPATIAL DATA   One of the three kinds of data (spatial, textural, and image). Spatial data is categorized according to the following feature types:

- Zero-dimensional features: primitive points; topological node
- One-dimensional features: primitive lines, strings (multiple nonbranching lines), arcs (mathematically defined curves), topological links, chains, and rings
- Two-dimensional features: polygons defining enclosed areas, pixels, and grid cells

SPATIAL QUERY   Function that allows a user to find, display, and/or isolate attributes records linked to map features located within a defined area of interest—window, circle, polygon, or trace.

SQL Acronym for Structured Query Language, a computer industry-standard syntax language for querying and manipulating most relational database management systems (DBMS). Commands can be embedded within a programming language to interface with a database, or can be used interactively.

STAGED PRECISION STRATEGY Process whereby, as much as possible, cost of developing engineering-design precision for each spatial feature is distributed over time. Adequate survey control network for the entire project area is a mandatory requirement. Once in place, conversion of map documents into digital format is performed on a best-fit basis. Such precision enhancements occur during the implementation of the following tasks/projects.

- Improvement/Development
- Land Transfer
- Land Valuation.

STATE PLANE COORDINATE SYSTEM System of X,Y coordinates defined by the U.S. Geological Survey (USGS) for each state. Locations are based on the distance from an origin point defined for each state, and are often split into multiple zones.

SURFACE Boundary of a three-dimensional figure. Two-dimensional locus of points located in three-dimensional space. Set of continuous data in which there is an infinite set of values between any two locations. Themes can be built from regularly or irregularly spaced sample points on the surface.

TCP/IP Transmission Control Protocol/Internet Protocol: protocol used by the Internet

THEMATIC MAP Representation of an area portraying how one or more real features or theoretical concepts are distributed. See also Coverages.

1. Displays a distribution of attributes. Typically a single variable (univariate) map such as for soil or land use. Can also depict ranges of calculated values like:
   Value category (i.e., 10–20% slope)
   Density (10–20 persons per acre)
   Relative suitability scores

2. Graphic display parameters typically include color assignment, solid fills, hatch patterns, symbols, and other graphic techniques.
3. Uses information stored in a spreadsheet or database to create map displays for graphic presentations.

THEMATIC PRECISION   A level of map accuracy used to describe graphic features needed to support multiple applications. (i.e., land base that supports a management system, land use and/or infrastructure master plans, or environmental impact assessments). A recommended standard could be all control points having an absolute accuracy of 5 feet or better and all referenced points having a relative accuracy of 20 feet or better.

THEME   Set of related geographic features, such as streets, parcels, or rivers, and their attributes (characteristics of those features). Geographic features logically organized into groups. Thematic map emphasizing a single environmental aspect, such as soils, land cover, or geology.

TIGER   Acronym for Topologically Integrated Geographic Encoding and Referencing; database standard developed by the U.S. Bureau of the Census to support the 1990 census.
1. Supersedes the original DIME file standard that had been applied to only portions of the United States
2. Introduces political boundaries, feature names, and ZIP code boundaries
3. Structured for easy implementation of standard address matching algorithms

TIN   Acronym for Triangulate Irregular Network, a representation of a plane surface as a grid of triangular polygons. Such models can be built into hierarchical structures and have a range of algorithms available for their formulation and translation to contour maps and surface grids.

TOPOLOGY   Relationships between spatial features, including such things as continuity, nearness, inside vs. outside, etc. Set of defined relationships between links, nodes, and centroids.
1. *Polygon Topology.* Representation of areas and area relationships using links and enclosed areas

2. *Network Topology.* Representation of a linear network by links and nodes

UNION A set, every member of which is an element of one or another of two or more given sets. The combination of two spatial data sets where the result includes all of the features of the two inputs.

UNIX Industry standard operating system (OS) developed as a joint venture between the University of California at Berkeley and the AT&T Bell Laboratories. A multiuser multitasking OS operates on a wide variety of computer systems, ranging from micro to mainframe. Written in C, it carries with it C's inherent transportability that enables it to be easily ported to many different hardware platforms. In addition to their own proprietary operating systems, many hardware vendors offer UNIX as an auxiliary OS, further expediting the free flow of data between multiple hardware platforms.

USER INTERFACE Components of software that expedite its intuitive and competent use. Options for command input by computer users rather than typing instructions at the command line. User interface can take on many forms, including screen, pull-down and pop-up menus; icons, dialog buttons, toggles and picklists; toolbar buttons; printed tablet menus and cursor buttons on digitizing (mouse) devices. Also includes productivity enhancements, error messages, error trapping, on-line help, MACROS (and their prompts), sample databases, tutorials, manuals, and other documentation.

UTILITY NETWORK A network topology particularly well suited for simulating utility operations.
1. *Pressure (Looping) Network.* A nonbranching utility network operation driven by position settings assigned to each end of each connecting link. Typical pressure networks include gas, water, and electric utilities.
2. *Gravity (Branching) Network.* Network database in which flow direction within a link is a determinate. All linear features are "drawn" according to their real-world direction to better support gravity network simulation transactions. Pertains particularly to sewer, storm, telephone, cable, and some electric utility networks.

VECTOR Method for storing spatial data involving assigning coordinates for each entity.

1. Mathematical object with precise direction and length but without specific location. Vector data is stored as XYZ coordinates that describe points, symbols, lines, areas, and volumes.
2. Method for storing spatial data involving assigning coordinates for each entity; an X,Y,Z for a point, a pair of such points for a line, a series of such lines for a polygon. The method is very useful for modeling discrete physical features.
3. Quantity, such as velocity, completely specified by a magnitude and a direction.

VIEWER A read-only stand-alone software system that supports the display, manipulation, and query of spatial databases. Commercial products that enable users to reference and analyze spatial databases prepared by a full function read-write product within the same product line. Typically has a user interface simpler than those of full function products. Supports rich command set, but less than that available in the full function product. Easily programmable to expedite establishment of read-only application.

VIEWSHED ANALYSIS Analytical technique to determine the area of the earth's surface that can be viewed from a particular vantage point.

VIRTUAL MAP Digital spatial database composed of multiple layers of specific area definitions, area boundaries, scale, features, related digital data files, and various other details selected as needed. Stored as a set of descriptive definitions that can be applied to create a map display on a pen plotter or an image on the screen, along with nongraphic data and instructions linked to various classes of map features.

VIRTUAL REALITY Spatial computing environment that enables users to interface with a spatial database in an intensive manner. Goggles are placed in front of the eyes, each lens of which is a computer screen displaying a view of a shaded 3-D spatial model (a building interior, urban plaza, a human knee joint, etc.) from a slightly different point of view. This displacement of viewpoints is equal to that between two human eyes, making it possible to perceive the spatial model comparably to the way the real world is viewed. Sensors in the goggles manipulate the model display so that it reflects what is seen as the user turns his head or moves his body. In addition, a glove and/or other devises that respond to movements make it possible for the user to manipulate objects within this virtual reality. Potential and standard practical applications are being implemented in the space program, surgery, and industrial processes.

INTRODUCTION

The enclosed CD-ROM contains a library of the graphics featured in the book. The graphics and accompanying summary text are provided in Portable Document Format (PDF) and must be viewed with Adobe Acrobat Reader 3.0 or higher. Adobe Acrobat Reader 3.0 for Windows and Adobe Acrobat Reader 3.0 for Macintosh are included on the CD-ROM.

MINIMUM SYSTEM REQUIREMENTS

Adobe Acrobat Reader 3.0 for Windows—System Requirements

- IBM or compatible PC with 386 or higher processor
- Microsoft Windows 3.1, Windows 95, or Windows NT 3.51 or later
- 8 MB of RAM (16 MB for Windows NT)
- 6 MB of hard disk space
- CD-ROM drive

Adobe Acrobat Reader 3.0 for Macintosh—System Requirements

- Macintosh with a 68020 or higher processor, or Power Macintosh
- Apple System Software version 7.0 or later
- 8 MB RAM

- 7 MB of hard disk space
- CD-ROM drive

ADOBE ACROBAT 3.0 INSTALLATION

Adobe Acrobat 3.0 is required to run this program. If you already have Acrobat Reader 3.0 or Exchange 3.0 (or later) on your computer, you should launch Acrobat Reader and choose File, Open. Select the file TBLOFCON.PDF in the graphics folder on your CD-ROM drive.

If you do not have Acrobat Reader or Exchange, or if your version is earlier than 3.0, follow the instructions below for your system.

Windows 95 or NT:

1. From the Start button, choose Run.
2. Type D:\ACROREAD\WIN\32BIT\SETUP.EXE (where D is the letter of your CD-ROM drive).
3. After the Reader installation is complete, launch Acrobat Reader and choose File, Open. Select the file D:\GRAPHICS\TBLOFCON.PDF (where D is the letter of your CD-ROM drive).

Windows 3.1:

1. From the Windows File Manager, choose Run from the File menu.
2. Type D:\ACROREAD\WIN\16BIT\SETUP.EXE (where D is the letter of your CD-ROM drive).
3. After the Reader installation is complete, launch Acrobat Reader and choose File, Open. Select the file D:\GRAPHICS\TBLOFCON.PDF (where D is the letter of your CD-ROM drive).

Macintosh:

1. Double-click on the Installer icon in the ACROREAD : MAC folder.
2. After the Reader installation is complete, launch Acrobat Reader and choose File, Open. Select the file TBLOFCON PDF in the GRAPHICS folder on your CD-ROM drive.

OPTIONAL: COPYING THE FILES TO YOUR HARD DRIVE

The installation as described above requires that you insert the CD-ROM each time you want to run the program. By copying the PDF files to your hard drive, you can view the files without the CD-ROM. In addition, this will modestly increase the program's speed of operation. To copy the files to your hard drive, do the following:

1. Create a new folder on your hard drive with any name you wish.
2. Copy the folder GRAPHICS and its contents, from the CD-ROM to your new folder.
3. Launch Acrobat Reader and choose File, Open. Select the file TBLOFCON.PDF in the GRAPHICS folder in your new folder on your hard drive.

USER ASSISTANCE

For more information about installing the Adobe Acrobat Reader, see the README files in each installer directory on the CD-ROM. For help using Acrobat Reader once it is installed, see the Reader Help menu. You can also get more information from the Adobe Web site at http://www.adobe.com.

If you have basic questions about using the CD-ROM, contact Wiley Technical Support at:

Phone: (212) 850-6753
Fax: (212) 850-6800
         Please send faxes to the attention of Wiley Technical Support.
E-mail: techhelp@wiley.com

To place additional orders or to request information about other Wiley products, please call (800) 225-5945.

CADD, *See* Computer Aided Drafting and Design
Calibration, 189–190
California, 57
CAMA (Computer Aided Mass Appraisal), 190
CAMA Interface Direct Query Application (CIDQA), 190
Canadian Land Inventory System, 15
Capability models, 83–84
Cartesian coordinates, 190
Cartography, 190
CAST, *See* Center for Advanced Spatial Technologies
Cells, 190
Census data, 190–191
Center for Advanced Spatial Technologies (CAST), xii, xv
Centerlines, 191
Centroids, 191
Character strings, 191
Chicago, 13
CIDQA (CAMA Interface Direct Query Application), 190
Clean data, 191
Client/server, 191–192
Clients using GIS, 101–103
COGO, *See* Coordinate Geometry
Commercial off-the-shelf (COTS) software, 177
Committing to GIS, 181–183
Common sense checks, 69
Composite mapping, 192
Computer Aided Drafting and Design (CADD), 7, 11, 18, 93–94, 96, 163, 167–168
    converting data from, 107–108
    in digital design process, 153, 158–161
    flat surfaces in, 8–9
    investing in, 33
    similarities of, to GIS, 35–36
    and site inventory, 132–133
Computer Aided Drafting (CAD), 189, 192
Computer generated maps, 104–105
Computer models, 48–49
Computers/computerization, 5, 6, 15, 17–18
    and design ability, 178
    fear of, 92–94
    microcomputers, 201
    minicomputers, 201
Conditions, negative vs. positive, 139
Conflation, 192
Conformal projection, 192
Conic projection, 192

Connectivity, 192
Conservation Foundation, 15
Construction documents, digital, 166
Continuous maps, 193
Contour mapping, 193
Contours, 10–11, 65–66
Conversion, 193
Coordinate Geometry (COGO), 192
Corridor analysis, 193
Costs of GIS, 34–35
COTS (Commercial off-the-shelf) software, 177
Coverage, 193
Crude data, 34
Culpepper, xiii, xiv
Cultural elements (in site inventory), 123
Cultural themes, 10
Curvature of the earth, 9
Cylindrical projection, 193

Data, 51–59, 193–194
    clean, 191
    commercial off-the-shelf, 54
    converting, from CADD, 107–108
    crude, 34
    digital, 195
    from federal collectors, 52
    homegrown, 53
    local collection of, 55–56
    metadata, 54–55, 201
    and quality control, 54
    remotely sensed, 169–172
    spatial, 207
    statewide, 52–53, 56–58
    suspicious, 58
    traditional methods of collecting, 51
    visualization of, 168–169
Database-initiated analysis operators, 63
Database Management Systems (DBMS), 8, 9, 47–48, 194
    records in, 194
Databases, 7–8, 168–169
    design of, 194
    hierarchical, 198
    relational, 9–10, 47, 204
    robust, 10
Data types, 10
Datum, 194
DBMS, *See* Database Management Systems
Decision matrices, 117–118
Decision support system, 194–195
Defense Mapping Agency, 21, 54
Definition of GIS, 33
Demographic, 195
DEMs, *See* Digital Elevation Models
Density map, 195

For information about the disk, refer to page 213.